J

ON THE
SIDE OF THE
ANGELS

By the same author

ON THE SIDE OF THE ANGELS

The Second Volume of the
Journals of Elizabeth Smart

EDITED BY ALICE VAN WART

HarperCollins*Publishers*

HarperCollins*Publishers*
77–85 Fulham Palace Road,
Hammersmith, London w6 8jb

Published by HarperCollins*Publishers* 1994
1 3 5 7 9 8 6 4 2

A catalogue record for this book is
available from the British Library

ISBN 0 246 13654 5

Set in Linotron Baskerville by
Rowland Phototypesetting Ltd
Bury St Edmunds, Suffolk

Printed and bound in Great Britain by
HarperCollinsManufacturing Glasgow

Only in as much as my life or anything
in my life corresponds to true things in other
people's lives is it of interest, and this depends
on telling the deep truths, and the surface facts
are just relieving frills, a few little restful
thrills, a bit of colour in the bare garden

Elizabeth Smart

CONTENTS

LIST OF ILLUSTRATIONS

(Courtesy of Georgina Barker unless otherwise stated)

PREFACE

Necessary Secrets, *the early journals of Elizabeth Smart, was published shortly after her death in 1986. Since that time, Smart's reputation has increased significantly enough to warrant a major biography and a documentary film of her life.* Necessary Secrets *traces the burgeoning of the writer up to 1941, the point at which Smart found herself in Pender Harbour, British Columbia, pregnant and, she believed, deserted by her lover, the poet George Barker. During this time she was working on* By Grand Central Station I Sat Down and Wept. *She finished it two weeks before the birth of her first child Georgina Barker on August 28, 1941.* On the Side of the Angels, *the second volume of her journals, begins at this point.*

For Smart life and art were inextricably connected. What she recorded in her journals was later culled for her work. She was never without a notebook. Even during the years she was a single mother with four young children, working in advertising to support them, with little time left over for journal writing, there were still notebooks full of lists, recipes, appointments, ideas, notes for commercial writing, drafts of articles, and book reviews. Smart thought of her journals as her writing apprenticeship and out of them came her classic By Grand Central Station I Sat Down and Wept *(1945), her later prose work* The Assumption of the Rogues and Rascals *(1978), the poems in* A Bonus *(1977) and the unpublished work collected in* In the Meantime *(1985).*

As well, Smart's journals reflect her life. The journals of the early forties articulate the desperation of a woman who has been left alone with children. The later journals show her struggle to go 'down deep', to speak what she called 'the truth' of herself and the frustrations of not being able to write.

From 1948 until the mid seventies, there are only sporadic journal entries, the lack of which attests to the fact that Smart was writing commercially to make a living. From 1950 until the mid seventies, Smart's notebooks are mostly small address books and appointment books that record the comings and goings

*of people to and from her various homes. She wrote little in her diary throughout
this period until the mid seventies, when she was able to resume extensive
journal writing again.*

*Smart's middle and late journals show no real interest in the creation of
character and event. Her focus has shifted from her earlier preoccupation with
love, passion and betrayal, as expressed in* By Grand Central Station I
Sat Down and Wept, *to the concerns of a woman coming to terms with her
life and her continuing struggle to write, as expressed in* The Assumption
of the Rogues and Rascals. *There is a consequential shift both in these
works and in her journals from the highly metaphoric style of the earlier work
to the more elliptical and aphoristic style, and philosophical and compassionate
viewpoint of the later work.*

*On the whole Smart transcended the impulse merely to document or to confess
in her journals. The preoccupation with the self is not an attempt to mythicize
or aggrandize it, but to explore it; as she says, 'to put it all down because of
all the other drowning women to whom no one has ever thought it worthwhile
to speak, or to whom no one would speak'.*

*For Smart writing was both spiritual and sexual. She believed in the muse,
in the act of being overtaken by words. She refers to the act of writing as
a fertilization of muse and words; there is a gestation period and then the
giving birth. The gestation for Smart was always long and the giving birth
painful. A single thread runs through Smart's journals and that is her difficulty
in being able to write. Throughout her life, Smart remained troubled over
the issue of creativity, particularly that of women, who, if they wished
to write, must obey both nature and the muse. Smart believed profoundly in
both and to the end of her life she would attempt to obey the imperatives of
each.*

*In editing these middle and late journals, I have stuck to the same principles
as I did in the early journals, which is to include only what seems to me the
important elements relating to Smart's writing and her inner life. My cutting
has been extensive and my focus remains on the literary. Again, I have cut the
poetry, the lists (Smart was a compulsive list-maker), all rough notes for her
extensive commercial writing and book reviews. Consequently the journals lose
much of their texture.*

*I continue to provide brief biographical commentary between sections, which
I have divided into decades. I have identified only those people who had importance in Smart's life and provided footnote material only when necessary. I
have tried to keep such apparatus to a minimum. I have tampered as little as*

possible with Smart's prose, but at times I have tightened up the syntax and written out all ampersands.

The extracts selected may produce some errors in transcription and dating. Smart's handwriting is difficult and she usually had more than one notebook at hand. Often dates within notebooks overlap. There are also sixteen undated notebooks. When no date has been given or I have not been able to identify a word I have indicated so (with N.D. and [illegible], respectively). I have used ellipses to indicate cuts between passages.

All extracts of journal material have been taken from Elizabeth Smart's notebooks housed in the Literary Manuscript Division of the National Library of Canada, in Ottawa. There are in all 158 notebooks and 111 of these are dated after 1941.

I would like to express my gratitude to Lorna Knight at the National Library, whose cataloguing of the large Smart collection is invaluable to future Smart scholarship, and to Kim Yates, who persevered in transcribing both Smart's and my own difficult handwriting. I would also like to thank the University of Toronto for giving me a project grant.

Alice Van Wart
Toronto 1992

I

THE FORTIES

From January 3 to July 12, 1942, Smart was in Washington working as a file clerk for the British Army Office. In April she brought her daughter Georgina (GEB), whom she had left in the care of her friend Maxie (Maximiliane Southwell) in Pender Harbour, B.C., to Washington. In May her application to extend her temporary stay in Washington was denied and she was asked to leave her post. During this time, George Barker was seeing both Smart and his wife Jessica.

Smart decided to leave Barker. In March 1943 through personal connections she got herself on a war convoy – her ship was torpedoed – and sailed for London, where a job had been secured for her in the Ministry of Information. She never started this job because it was discovered she was pregnant.

Barker soon followed Smart to England although he had still not officially left Jessica, who was now also pregnant. On July 23, 1943, Christopher Barker was born to Elizabeth Smart and on August 27, 1943, Anthony and Anastasia Barker were born to Jessica Barker.

Smart briefly settled in the Cotswolds, in College Farm, Condicote, close to her friend Didy Asquith and her children. In May 1944 Smart's father died unexpectedly. A year later Sebastian Barker was born, on April 16, 1945, and By Grand Central Station I Sat Down and Wept *was being published. Two days after the birth of Sebastian, and still in hospital, she received the proofs of* By Grand Central Station I Sat Down and Wept. *For the second time child and book came together. When six copies of this book were shipped to Ottawa, Smart's mother bought them and burned them. She then had the book censored.*

In July 1946, pregnant again, Smart moved her family to Ireland in an attempt to end her relationship with Barker. Barker arrived at Shannon airport in September. Rose Barker was born on February 18, in County Galway. Barker, who had already returned to England, did not see Rose until she was six and a half months old.

At the end of June, with her emotional and financial resources depleted, Smart returned to England. Now, with the help of her sister Jane, she rented Tilty Mill House in Essex. During the next two years George Barker came and went. Smart kept a log of his visits and the length of time he stayed.

As a single mother with four young children, Smart desperately needed a job. She began free-lance writing, and in 1949 she was hired by House & Garden *as a subeditor. Full-time work relieved Smart's financial worries, but it meant that her children had to be sent to boarding schools. During the week Smart now worked in London and spent weekends with her children at Tilty Mill.*

The forties notebooks are full of lists, lists of what is needed and of what is on hand, lists of books read by her children and books she wishes them to read. They are full of recipes, accounts, and debts. There is the beginning of a biography of George Barker and in a 1945 journal she lists every review or notice given to Barker's poetry. There is also 'A Guidebook to Barker's Babies', which she wrote for the help she had to look after the children. There are only sporadic journal notes from 1946 to 1949.

December 31, 1941, 'Memoranda'

This was a very sad year for ES – it was spent mostly in having Georgina – and the very great joy of it was turned into the worst imaginable sorrow.

> 'I came too late in time
>
>   etc.'

It is really too terrible to record.

October 19, 1942

Therapeutics
Healing games
This way. That way – madness lies.
      Pamper.
      Humser. The madman.
But take away his tools.
(O for the touch of his salty lip.)
And he lay arced above her unclean core.
And in how many shitholes has he buried the key to my
fulfilment.

And though I say 'I', I know that I achieve this pillar of quality by being sent to try him and make him absolutely mine. O bring repetition.

Continuity lacking.
Fear invading. I am doodling with my mind.
There is no urgency.
George has hardened his heart.
He is mad.
I am mad too, with an inward curtain-like madness. A pall.
There is no illumination.

I have children. But I have ceased to care about anything. I have no personal ambition, or even the desire that people call me nice, or pretty, or witty. Nor do I have any use for sensation, nor do I care. Cessation. It is a technical circling, encircling, cycle, of giving the body to be burned, but having no charity.

When the raids come, I am not very much afraid, but merely afraid. Not saying, O let us die together, in each other's arms. No, for George naps through all, and my arms are not his comfort and his home.

True, he is harassed by joblessness and cashlessness, but if I were harassed and had external trouble it would be love I would crave to cool my forehead with.

[Section deleted]

What can I do? For without love I am truly dead. Will it awake in him and be renewed like the spring? Probably not now. (O, but I don't believe this. If I did, why would I dare get up and walk down the streets? No. I am merely bitter.)

He sees now in everything I do ulterior and reprehensible motives: I waste my fare, even 'for the wrong reasons'.

(Sir. cf. Jessie: that noble creature who also tells herself that she can't believe in the bad motives of anyone else! Balls.)

Balls to you, Jessica, with your astute love of the abused. The reason you manage him so cleverly is because you don't love him. He's *your* husband and *your* honour is at stake. You like the pose of the faithful wife. Besides, you anticipate prizes. (Now you're being vulgar, Elizabeth. O then will the psychoanalyst judge? No, he will say: Tell me what you are afraid to tell me: Well, mother said I must never call anyone common.)

December (ND)

Madness is perfection.

No, perfection is madness.

His potion for perfection is proof of his madness. His madness was caused by his passion for perfection.

You are passionate but you are not perfect. I know. I know. I am mad but I am not passionately seeking perfection. I am not seeking passion either. I am corseted by fear. I can't move. I am mad with fear. Fear has driven me mad. I am afraid of the wind, the empty house, the air-raids, burglars, lunatics, ghouls, catastrophe, sudden appearances, disappearances, death. O I am afraid of death. I am most afraid of death.

He can get me but I can't get him.

Do I want to record these days? These purgatorial days which I forget even before they are gone?

George, you must do something. I CAN'T stay alone in this house for so many hours. I AM GOING MAD.

Where are you? It is nearly 9. You said you would be here at 5. You said you loved me. You said you'd rather be at home than out and about. I am frightened. I am lonely. I am miserable. I am empty. I think I may die. I can't read or pray or think or write or sew or relax or wash my hair or go about the house putting it into place.

Is there something everybody knows and I don't know?

June 17, 1943

I picked these summer roses because they looked so disgusting waiting there desperately wanting the bees to come and fuck them.

On this lonely afternoon what is left of my youth gushes up like a geyser as I sit in the sun combing the lice out of my hair.

For it is difficult to stop expecting ('what my heart first waking whispered the world was') even though I am a woman of $31\frac{1}{2}$ with lice in my hair and a faithless lover.

It is June 17 but the sun keeps going in and I have been frustrated too many times to be able to withstand its uncertainty. Who can I talk to? To whom can I show off my brilliance and my newly-brightened age or the cynicism I have made out of my despair instead of a dreary moaning and groaning?

Last night the pressure of my captivity and my helplessness made my brain reel, so that I felt dizzy and faint. Rats and rabbits die of indecision when an experiment forces them to be forced two ways. Why shouldn't I die at the insolubility of my problems and the untenability of my position?

I need a house, a husband, money, a job, friends, furniture, affection, servants to look after the children, clothes, a car, a bicycle, a destination. Who is there for me? I see now I was the one-too-many. I was the mistake. The circumstances in which I find myself are marginal notes, never the text. It will revert to the simple narrative, what it was when it started, before I entered, far, far too positive of getting my just share.

In the thick hedgerows the summer flowers like their rapturous lives that have nothing to do with me.

N.D.

The perennial vines weeping along the wall in spite of summer remind me of the empty road where I persevere always and at last, always out of reach, out of hearing, when the Act is enacted.

Yet I have listened as attentively as most and have been ready to be helpful to history or live as epitome. I expect that perhaps I was overeager like the scarred or outcast woman to whom all men and all circumstances say Be off cloying and clawing for I will be after the fickle whore. Like [illegible]. O too too much like [illegible].

N.D.

If he had the faculty of memory, could anything that has happened have happened? And if there are never any memories that can make the paper burn, how can any words of mine expect his heart to melt?

Poor women with their lost souls and their hopeless causes. Poor world with its security anxieties, literally dying for prestige, for beggar my neighbour, for pride, for vanity. Is it worth it being involved again?

And yet I must put it all down because of all the other drowning women to whom no one has ever thought it worthwhile to speak, or to whom no one would speak.

January 10, 1944: To George.

There are (for me) two things on which it was all founded: (a) I love you; and (b) you are a poet: both of these are still true.

But as for (b): I and my children contribute nothing whatsoever towards your being a poet: you will be one whether we exist or don't exist, with us or without us. On the other hand, if your Jessie skins her knee you can be moved to elegies and write a cycle of lullabies if she has diarrhoea.

As regards (a), I am obviously not loved in return, nor needed, and I cannot bear to be by and watch the object of my love ignoring me, abusing me, insulting me, everyday forgetting the reason why we even met. I don't feel you have any respect for me, nor any consideration and if I continue to live in the radius of your hate and disregard, I shall lose my own self-respect, what's left of it.

We are obviously the supernumerary: You don't need us. Therefore for our own sakes, we must Get Out of it altogether and leave you with what's yours in all senses of the word, what moves you and what, if anything, you love: I mean Jessie and her two wrong-reason twins. Perhaps she loves you enough to carry water and wash dirty nappies and cook and sweep and sit up alone night after night, or perhaps you love her enough to help her when she needs it and to want to be with her occasionally. Anyhow; as you say, the crux of every matter is cash and she has always been able to get cash out of you and evidently always will, even if she has to get the Foreign Office to pursue you: while I have never been able to get a penny, a poem or a word of praise.

So now alas and farewell, you whose true wife I would rather have been than had all the other prizes besides.

I am very bitter and very angry and very full of hate and revenge, but I knew too well the moment you closed the door that the love is not to be destroyed. It really is IN DESPITE. And though tonight I sat down to write you a reasonable list of reasons why I must leave you (or 'we must part' if you insist on pedantry), I find my pencil keeps wanting to write a love letter. This is because of (a) I love you, I guess. But if I *only* loved you, I would not for a moment have tolerated the abuse, the selfishness and calmness and betrayals for a moment . . .

*

January 16, 1944

I am not the bride. Life lies on top of me like the refuse of the world. Love lies inside like a forgotten bullet from a forgotten war.

May 9, 1944

We are at College Farm, Condicote. It was a nice sunny day, less cold than usual, nearly hot enough. George and I are sick with strange things wrong in our insides. And besides this, everything is wrong with our life, since George spends all his time plotting to get to America and I sense if he does we forever part. What sort of a foundation is there for a peaceful domestic life? I don't see why he hasn't the honesty to face this fatal discrepancy, as it would surely make things easier for all of us.

May 10, 1944

The doctor (J. E. Jameson) came just after teatime to look at Giffy's [Christopher Barker] vaccination and it's taken perfectly. But after tea, Giffy threw up all his tea and his lunch and got a high colour. Didy came over earlier to ask us to go and meet the Asquiths (Herbert and Cynthia) at 5:30. George walked over and I went later on the bicycle. Didy[1] went to [illegible] and motored them there to have dinner and we stayed and had baths. When we got back here, Mrs Foster said Giffy had been sick again and she had changed him.[2]

May 11, 1944

Giffy had a high fever and flaming colour. Didy saw him and George went over to get Glucotin from her. Giffy had nothing but Glucotin all day. I was very worried and hated George because he resented that I hadn't swept the floor. Giffy wouldn't let me leave him and I had to rock his bed to put him to sleep.

In the evening I mended and George went over to Didy's for a while. [illegible] Westwood was there. (George bicycled to Stow-on-the-Wold to get glucose.)

May 12, 1944

Giffy all better and terribly hungry. After lunch, George bicycled to Moreton-in-Marsh and after their rests I took the children along the road to meet him. Mrs Foster ironed and starched all Georgina's dresses. After supper we went to Didy's and talked for a long time. A lovely hot day.

May 13, 1944

Domestic day. Didy came for the tea urn from Mrs Foster. Some-one turned on the top of her beer barrel and five gallons of beer for the christening flowed away.

May 14, 1944

In the evening we walked to Longborough, and I had 1½ pints of cider and was nicely drunk. On the way home I dashed into the prickles because George made a tit-for-tat remark about dedicating his book *Eros in Dogma*[3]. (He 'didn't consult Jessica when he dedi-cated his book to me'.) I lay among the prickles along the hedge and wanted to cease. When I got home, George was having supper and reading. He got into bed, and neither of us said anything, except George who made a few caustic remarks. But when I got into bed we made love.

May 16, 1944

George went off on his bicycle to go to [illegible] to catch the train to London. Georgina cried brokenheartedly. She's consoling herself with 'George's going to bring me a present'. After he had gone she stamped her feet and screamed. And she kept remembering intermittently. If rocked. Didy and Susan Asquith came for a few moments. I was glad to go to bed early. Two boxes came from Mummy this morning. Sleepers for Giffy, underthings for Georgina, a green sweater for me.

May 17, 1944

Cold, wet and blowy. Georgina watched the thrashing. All the children have big sticks and kill the rats and mice with gusto. Didy came out before lunch with Annabel, and just before tea with Vivian John. But she never stays more than a minute or two. I served and mended. Ate cocoa and read, but I couldn't get the fire going satisfactorily.

I realize that I am afraid to say the important things and therefore there seems little point in this book except an exercise in description

and daily domestic details. Perhaps one thing will lead to another –
or the truth will emerge from the omissions.

May 18, 1944

A lovely day. Didy and Annabel came to tea (all her guests have
left) and actually sat through a few minutes. About 8:30 I walked
over in my moccasins (all my other shoes having collapsed) and got
Didy out of bed (she had given me up) and sat talking until midnight. I rode home on Roger's bicycle. It was very dark and I felt
very sad and tired.

May 19, 1944

A lovely sunny morning. Didy came early for the bicycle. I sat
out with the children mending my blue striped dress. Giffy had on
his blue corduroy overalls and a sunbonnet and Georgina her
starched seersucker dress. After lunch as I was hurrying to get the
things ready to take on the picnic a woman on a bicycle stopped
and said, 'Can you tell me where College Farm is?' and she had two
telegrams one for Mrs Barker and one for Elizabeth Smart. I said,
'They're both for me.' One was from Harry at the bank saying
Daddy has died yesterday and the other was from Bobby saying
how sorry she was.[4] It was bewildering and too much of a shock to
believe. I cried but then began agitatedly getting the picnic things
together, and crying. And thought, all one can do after all *is* to cry.
It doesn't seem enough. But I tried not to give myself time to realize
it because I didn't want to collapse at the picnic or have to tell them.
Nannie was there and we sat in the bluebell wood and I picked a
bunch of orchids and Annabel let Georgina play with her big doll
and pram. And of course the more things flowered the more sad it
seemed and the meaner more horrible death and I know that I am
guilty because Daddy had me so much on his mind and I did always
so much make him part of me and happy, and he was so optimistic.
And now things really have fallen apart and how can the centre
hold. Harry's wire said one from Mummy was being sent with a
letter. I can feel the taste of death in my own mouth. But there is
never and nowhere a time for such a word.

A form came for George from the American consul to emigrate to
America to 'join his wife and children'.

The evening by myself was horrible.

May 20, 1944

A wire from Charlie Ritchie[5] saying Russel Smart arriving in Condicote this afternoon. I spent ages phoning bank to leave a message. I took the children to Didy to lunch and tea. We sat talking but I didn't tell her. George got back just after we did. I sent him (tiffs and huffs) to Didy's for supper and waited for Russel, but a message came saying he'd missed his train and would be down tomorrow. So I cycled over to Didy's and joined them.

[Section deleted]

May 30, 1944

Georgina and I went with Didy to Moreton. Georgina insisted on wearing her fancy dress hat. We shopped. (I cashed a £2 2s 0d check from George.) We went back to Didy's for lunch and George brought Giffy over in the pram. We sat in the garden in the sun all afternoon. Georgina very tense from Annabel's using her pram with her toys over her. Tea in the garden and I bathed the children in the kitchen sink. Didy drove us home. Mrs Foster had saved us a hot supper. We read.

June 5, 1944

My overdraft is only £44 18s 4d

Cold and wet.

Christopher has a cold, and I am all aches with one coming on. At noon Didy stopped at the window in one of the big cars with Annabel lying tiny in the back with Nannie, and she said, 'Annabel's just had an operation but she's all right.' George said, 'What on earth's the matter?' but she said, 'I'll tell you all about it this evening.'

George went over in the evening – I had a cold so I couldn't. George said Didy'd be hurt but I said she wouldn't like me going with a cold. He said, 'You talk a lot of balls.' I was hurt (inwardly). I got into bed with hot cocoa and a hot water bottle and a flannelette nightgown and a [illegible] book after having an enema. It was my first luxuriousness for ages. I was asleep when George got back, but woke up. All night the planes were going.

June 6, 1944

Mrs Foster knocked on the door and said, 'Mrs Barker, the

invasion has started.' We saw dozens and dozens of planes with gliders going off in the evening. Against impressive grey clouds in the cold. I made an orange tunic for Georgina out of an old skirt from Didy and half one for Christopher. My cold is maddening. I can't breathe and I ache all over. George bicycled over to Didy's to get some Benzedrine. I went to bed to nurse my cold with Mummy's dehydrated chicken soup and [illegible] short stories.

June 8, 1944

Having a cold and going to bed early and being paralysed by the invasion. All the planes in the sky are so busy. All I seemed to do was read and blow my nose.

June 10, 1944

News from Ave dated May 21. I expected George (sort of) yesterday. At teatime I waited, thinking he might come. I lit the fire for the first time since he'd left. The coachman hasn't come and there's no fuel. When I went to see the time it was ten to eight. So I just dumped the children in bed. Alfred had gone by on his cart and said Didy would like to see me tonight. Vivian and Simon hadn't come, though they were expected yesterday and no word either. I went over on Mrs Foster's bicycle. Nannie was there but I went to the big house for a while.

I am going to leave George. Didy says she's come to the conclusion I should too. She says we are incompatible. I say Jessica is ideally suited to him, not me at all. Didy and I say we are, as they say of pilots, 'finished'. We quake at the sound of motors starting up. I am very sad, and I wonder if ever I will be strong enough.

June 12, 1944

Didy came over just as I was finishing the housework. I was scared by the planes zooming, banking and circling. But it was nothing. Georgina knew I was going and cried.

London

Benzedrine – George's ashen stiff face. Flying bombs. [illegible] with family because of G. Didy's tight shoes. [Vera?] and George and his pocketful of betrayals and repudiations escape me never. Next time, if it comes, what will I be asked to do but die?

June 26, 1944

It is raining. George's in London.

Didy and I were talking (children sleeping in the loft) when George phoned. He came back because of the flying bombs.

1945 'A Woman of Thirty's Law of Years'

Once upon a time a woman was wandering in the wastes of Kensington. The mean mad faces passed intermittently like derelict paperbags. The neat ruins of the war lie like a boring scar where history is all of the repetitious failure and all that memory can retain. It is the autumnal equinox that blows out the pleats of my tweed skirt. The moon races behind the tall and interminable wilderness of [illegible] Gardens.

N.D.

'Flesh sings a law of years from grief to grave.' (W S Graham, *Fifth Journey*).[6]

> Flesh sings a law of grief
> > of years
> > of going to the grave

June 28, 1944

Churchill is cunning. He is a liar.

He will get in.

This is the time I pity them.

They had so much sense. I wanted to weep. But they didn't hope. The Canadians hoped a bit, because of the 50,000 who trained in Canada, and their determination for change. But the South African said, 'I don't expect it to happen.'

N.D.

Mothers with shamed faces are slapping their babies for relief.

N.D.

If you do what you want to when you want to, then you will have to do what you don't want to when you don't want to. (Maxims of ES After love, while scribbling.)

N.D.

Now am I to govern every utterance, saying I must be careful, lest this appear egotistical? No.

June 28–July 4, 1944

All those days George sulking and hating me because I got an answer (harmless) from the letter I wrote Frampton July 6.[7] Nothing will ever be right until he wants more children, not necessarily *per se*, but necessarily and because of the nature of love. I know I know I know he's only trying to keep the situation OPEN for Jessica so his misinterpretations, (I mean lies) will work out. O hell. O Heaven. O horror and he expects me to take this merely marking time and call it love and be willing. Of course I can't really write in this book because he reads it and takes offence throwing up continually the fact that I wrote, 'I am going to leave George.' I know that I am not a wise woman, or I could wait wisely, or say nothing and never want to see his letters or know to whom he writes or what he does in London or how he feels about J. But it is four years ago today since we met, and it is still as messy, if not messier than ever. The trouble is, for me, that there is always *hope*, i.e. either J. is a wonderful woman, in which case a terrible solution might be possible, or she is not, and he might eventually realize it. As for me, I feel myself getting less and less wonderful, and I shall certainly *not* be able to make any more noble omissions, or stand any more chicaneries, or sit back while he stands on his head to get back his devotions. If only, even for this limited period, he were really given to me and loving me without always (wondering!) whether he'll be able to camouflage what he's doing.

New Year's Resolutions 1945
1) Keep a diary or Daily Notebook.
2) Keep Accounts and *never* spend more than £20 a month on living (and partly living).
3) Keep the children Prettily dressed always.
4) Keep Everything *Clean*.
5) Answer all letters within three days.
6) Keep bowels open.
7) Have a baby. [checked] Sebastian 16 April 1945.

8) Learn to play Chess.

9) Write Canadian History Book.

10) Acquire a Radio, Piano, Dulcitone, Harpsicord, Clavichord, gramophone or Alto as means of obtaining music, and teach children to listen.

11) Translate Canadian Folksongs and acquire all available books and information on them.

12) Make a final decision about George, if he won't about me, and stick to it. The years roll on and the freezing wind.

January 1, 1945

Facts: in bed at Didy's with only occasional airholes to breathe. Big fingers and thumbs behind eyes and nose and temples.

Smothering in luxurious white bed. Cold. Lovely outside. Reading. George in London.

January 5, 1945

Letter From G.

January 6, 1945

Went to Moreton from bed at Didy's to see Mr Barker, an EN&T specialist. He did a sinus operation with local anaesthetic. Rather exhilarating.

January 8, 1945

Giffy came with Big Girl and brought in a treacle treat and *Woman's World*. How can this be a real diary or any use at all if I am much too cowardly and lazy.

January 11, 1945

Jean brought me a maternity dress in grey blue and pants. I am all passion spent and can think of nothing exciting or worth doing.

January 12, 1945

Food parcel from [illegible], doll from Big Mumma[8] for Georgina and letter from George. He says nothing but what he's said for nearly five years. I don't feel hopeful. There's nothing concrete. The new leader's dull and has [illegible]. Georgina is very gay.

January 14, 1945

Georgina all spotty with chicken pox. I had her bed brought down here, so we are now one on either side of the fireplace. She's rather pale and whiny and restless. Pat here most of day and tonight. Supper with Fosters. Sewed names on vests and nappies.

January 15, 1945

Georgina awake (and me too) most of the night. Very hot head and pasty face. I play with her all the time. Didy and the children came for a minute after lunch and I took Giffy to post letters and saw Mrs Pilkerton and puppies. Giffy and Big Girl came to tea with Georgina and me. Sweater came from Vivien. Sewed on nametags and sat while Georgina slept.

January 18, 1945

Rained in the night, wind, rain and hail. It hangs about. I feel full of fluid and irritable. Remade a nightie for Giffy and altered blue tweeds for Georgina as I did for Giffy last night. Let her get in for half hour before bedtime. George didn't come. G.[eorgina] gay all day, but tonight rather subdued and wide-eyed and strange. Told me her fears about bombs, mice and the nursery. Can't make out whether they are real fears of her own, or fears put there by other people, i.e. Renee, or the Fosters, etc., sympathizing with her and frightening her. She said Annabel was afraid of mice. (I don't think G. really knows what a mouse is. So it must be other people's suggestions.) She looks sweet in navy blue tweed skirt ('skoit' she calls it.)

January 26, 1945

Phoned George. He unpleasant. I suggested going to London for weekend. He didn't want me at all. Spoke to Big Mumma. Didy came. Went to her home at 8 PM and stayed the night.

January 27, 1945

Went into Moreton to go to London. Didn't go. Too reluctant.

January 31, 1945

George came about six.

*

February 4, 1945
George got mad and I went over to Didy's and he left for London.

February 10, 1945
Went to prenatal clinic with Mrs P. and Georgina. Everything OK.

February 13, 1945
George phoned at bathtime.

February 20, 1945
We all caught 7:20 AM train to Oxford. Didy and Annabel got off, and G. and I went on. We were on a through train to London by mistake so had to change at Early and [illegible]. Reached Reading about 10:30 and caught a bus to Longtown Rd at 11:15. Jean met us and we had drinks in Bird in Hand with Jane Mitchell (the 'Colonel's Wife'). They let GEB into pub too. Hostess Mrs Dudley had bandana and paint. Jean's house octagonal with lots of windows and air and sun in top of the hill in the woods.

February 23, 1945
Caught 1:20 back to Reading and 2:35 train home. Spent night at Didy's. Letter from G. and parcel from Renee and book (from G).

February 26, 1945
George's birthday.

March 4, 1945
Overcast and rather bleak and raining. George went to pub in evening to get cigarettes. Psychologically overcast too. Sore throat. George's sores.

March 13, 1945
Very bad flu and bad cold.

March 15, 1945
Letter from George. Scrubbed floor. Got suitcase nearly ready.

*

March 23, 1945
George came.

March 27, 1945
I was weighed on Sunday and I am 13 stone. 58 pounds more than usual. Lovely spring weather. I am very heavy and full to bursting.

April 4–April 12, 1945
Vernal squall
I HATE the Vulgar Mob and SHUN them.
Hate Hate God God I could scream.

April 16, 1945
11:30 P.M. (British Double Summertime). Gave birth to Sebastian in Moreton Hospital.

April 26, 1945
It is unbearable loving George. I always *knew* he (wouldn't) couldn't come and yet I always expect him and sit in that insane fever of anticipation no matter how I keep telling myself his coming is out of the question. What can I possibly do? I really *can't* bear it. It gets worse, not better. He won't let me leave him, yet he won't stay with me. He won't settle my difficulties, and yet he won't let me try and settle them for myself. I love him desperately, but he continually ruins my hopes that we are going to lead a happy married life together. I *always* believe that this time it will really happen and there is never anything but the same disappointments and frustrations. He never comes when he says he will. He always stays away two or three times as long as he says he will. He always vanishes and lets me sit waiting for him in my best clothes, relishing the hour to come. O God George, can't you see that I can't bear this life of continual frustration and solitude? Suddenly one day I will crack, snap, break into bits and BE GONE.

September 27, 1946
I do not think that I want to lie down in your crowded bed for bouts of therapeutic lovemaking. Loving you, I see no beauty in lopsided true love. It really is in sorrow and not in anger that I say:

I do not want you any more because I *simply cannot bear it*. It isn't only the unfaithfulness. It's the loneliness, the weeks and months of being alone, really cut off from you, receiving perhaps a postcard saying fuck you as you pause for breath in fucking somebody else. It would have been better had I married before I met you, because then you could have given me a few months of fulfilling attentions, which is all, apparently, that women need, and then I could have returned to the someone who possibly would have cared for me. For you do not want the responsibility even of love and by this responsibility I do not mean either money or guilt.

I realize that if you had cared about me the small necessary amount you would not have left me alone with so much pain, but would have contrived to find some other way of doing what you had to. This is the depths and the final and the end of my misery and degradation and if I say goodbye to you now I will be able to keep from being bitter because I am so grateful to you for your last few moments of frankness.

Dearest George, I will NOT give up the belief in true love or if you will romantic love – IT IS possible. I KNOW. I never *wanted* anybody since you. IT IS possible to cometh to rest in someone – but you have not evidently had enough pleasure and power. Maybe I want the middle-aged things now. I've had my fuck, but I've lost my LOVE. My womb won't tear me to pieces now, maybe, but my heart certainly will. Goodbye. Elizabeth.

II

THE FIFTIES

The fifties for Smart began an intensely social period. Until 1954, when Tilty Mill was sold, Smart had worked in London during the week and on weekends returned to Tilty Mill with her children. She now moved her family to London, in 1955 settling in 9 Westbourne Terrace. Her home soon became the centre for various writers and artists. For a while the Scottish poet W S (Sydney) Graham rented a room. George Barker continued to appear, though he spent more and more time in Italy. His relationship with Smart was now one of friendship. Poet David Wright was a familiar figure at Smart's, as were two Scottish artists, Robert MacBryde and Robert Colquhoun, known as the Roberts, who were the children's nannies.

Although there was little time for Smart to write, in 1951 a story of hers titled 'The Assumption of the Rogues and Rascals', appeared in the prestigious Botteghe Oscur. *This story would later comprise Part Five of* The Assumption of the Rogues and Rascals. *The same journal published another story, 'A Simple Statement', in 1953.*

In 1954 Smart took a full-time job copywriting for Crawford's Advertising Agency. She also continued free-lance writing for House & Garden *and* Vogue. *Smart worked hard. She was a single mother providing for four children, each in a private school. In 1957, however, she managed to publish with her friend Oonagh Swift (who used the pseudonym Agnes Ryan)* Cooking the French Way *and in 1958 she began work on a biography of Marie Stopes, the pioneer campaigner for birth control. Although Smart did extensive research for the project, she did not complete it.*

Smart's working life was relieved by afternoons and evenings in Soho, gathering with friends in a few favourite pubs. In 1957 she visited her family in Ottawa and her sister Jane in Vermont and went to Paris with Barker.

During these years Smart's journals are mostly appointment books listing deadlines, appointments, the names of visitors at Tilty, and rough notes for her various writing projects. There are no full journal entries for 1956.

June 20, 1952

A) 'But look, Mrs Green, it can't have been as bad as that. Why, you girls had a wonderful childhood. Your parents kept open house. No one could have been kinder than your parents. You girls don't know how lucky you were. Your grandmother too. Why, Miss Kady used to come every Tuesday to put her hair in tight little snow white curls. She looked a picture.'

On the screened-in veranda where tea was served on a trolley with silver pot, cucumber sandwiches, cheese cakes, angel cakes, cookies, and cinnamon toast, sometimes the mournful tones of Bob Devlin's saxophone wafted through the talk, and the ladies were disturbed as if he had lurched into their midst. (He drinks, my dear, he drinks.) To a child such desperation coming across the lake explained itself. There perished an early pioneer, born in the wrong place, in the wrong time, without a furious weapon.

Well; *get* a furious weapon. Look how etc.

B) 'Poor little woman! That cough's killing her.'
   'Left with all them kiddies.'
   'Keeps them real clean, I will say that for her.'
   'No word from her husband?'
   'Not there five years.'
   'Can't they make him pay?'
   'No one knows where he is.'
   'Mum! Mum! Why is her nose so red?'
   'Sh! She's got a cold.'

C) Well, look around. Keep your eye on the object. Insist on a shape. Stagger out of the procreational slime. What size shoe does he take? How big is his collar? Who were her people? Where was the scene of the crime?[1]

Friday night and the clocks breathe freely. Intimations of wild other lives sway their limbs in barbarous rhythm. O to leap into chaos. By an amber whisky mist their faded brown eyes are shielded from the sight of their submission. The fathers throw all overboard and indeed they're wise to do so. Whose will summons the seven days set in spirals of whirling time? Not the worried burdened. It's enough if their breath holds out. Have you done the dishes? Is the fire still in? And all the while those kingcarps were in that watery part of the world. It's several months since you last looked out the window. There have been two litters of pigs and the village children are giggling into girls. The green is getting brownish like a maturing woman's skin. It's just genuine now, and serviceable. Don't look back. If you haven't used the spurt of spring, you'll have to wait till the year comes round. Go about your business. The blur of necessity will keep you trotting about. Yes, but their dying faces.

January 8, 1953
  To London with Bobby, Hugo and Roger
  11:15 Dentist
  3:00 *Vogue* – for March 'Shophound'
  H&G Colour DUE.
  Back by 8:22. A terrible day.

February 21, 1953
  GB left at 12. (WHY?)

February 26, 1953
  GB is 40 today.

November 9, 1953
  Dylan Thomas died. (Paul Potts[2] phoned 9:30 with news.)

February 22, 1954
  To Big Mumma's with Georgina and Paddy at lunchtime. Took parcels to Catherine's and then went to Big Mumma's to see Georgina and then to Oonagh's and Paddy's[3] to [illegible] their bath and bed.

March 2, 1954
  H&G feature editions at 1.
  1:30 George and Andy, French pub.
  5:30 Go to Big Mumma to see Rose then out with GB, Paddy.

April 12, 1954
  WSG at 1. Here to go to Bank.
  Dinner at home with Sydney and Nessie.

May 26, 1954

Lunch with David Archer at home.

To drinks with Trevelyans to see Yanko Varda after 14¾ years.[4]

June 5, 1954

Boys visiting for weekend, begins at noon. To Big Mumma's and then George drove us to Hampstead to fair (in rain) drinking there – all slept Hampstead.

August 28, 1954

Georgina is 13.

To Walton on the Naze. Left about 12 – picnic lunch at the beach (four children plus Olga and David Wright, Robert MacBryde, G. Spry and me).[5]

October 1, 1954

Joy at lunchtime. Ill in bed and Joy and Geoff and Derek but got up and went to Canada House (Mike Pearson and Charlie Ritchie). Dinner.[6]

December 5, 1954

GB came to tea and then we met Paddy and Oonagh in the Lamb and over to Mandrake and took rum back to Hampstead. Slept there. D[avid] and O[lga] Wright left Lamb early.

February 26, 1955

Very icy cold. GB's birthday. Went to park with Rosie and later to movie with her and [illegible]. In all evening.

April 17, 1955

GB to lunch and until after tea. Joy and Anthony to tea.

April 23, 1955

Rose and Georgina back to school. GB motored us to Tunbridge Wells and back. Drinks locally with GB, Walter and Roberts and all stayed the night.

May 21, 1955

David Archer phoned to say Big Mumma dead.

To French pub – eat noon.
Home to read.
Then to Queen's Slum, to Wendy's wedding party. All there.
To nightclub and then GB and me home.

October 30 to November 8, 1955
In bed ill.

November 9, 1955
Went to Paddington Hospital in ambulance. GB visited to November 14.

November 24, 1955
In bed again.

December 18, 1955
GB disappeared while I was in bath. Four children and me to see movie. Early bed.

December 27, 1955
GB disappeared.

February 2, 1957
Collect clothes from Liberty's.
9:30 – leave airport for Canada. The Roberts, Paddy, saw me off.
In Labrador for 1½ hours, in Montreal at dawn. Ottawa for lunch: Russel, ELS (Elizabeth) and JAS (Jane). To see Russel and Nancy and children.

February 14, 1957
To Vermont.

August 26–December 15, 1957
Spent with GB.

September 7, 1957
To Paris with GB.

*

September 14, 1957
  Back from Paris.

September 23, 1957
  Crawford's 4:15.
  In Colony at 6. Then drinking locally with GB.

September 26, 1957
  David Wright arrived early and GB went out with him drinking
and I joined him between CB [Cristopher Barker] [illegible] and
getting him home to tea etc.

October 4, 1957
  Down to cottage in GB's car with David Archer.

October 7, 1957
  10:45 Conde Nash and Crawford's. To Finchley in GB's car to
collect Roberts and [illegible]. Had drinks and dinner here, then
Soho.

December 7, 1957
  GB left late in huff with his radio.

December 25, 1957
  Tony Kingsmill for coffee. GB came for Christmas dinner about
3. Archer at teatime to Henrietta's with GB back alone.

December 27, 1957
  My Birthday
  To party at [illegible] with GB. Prunella drove us back.

January 5, 1958
  GB away.
  Roberts arrived and RC (Robert Colquhoun) had a sitting with
Susan Winslow.

February 26, 1958
  George is 45 and due in Oxford. We met at 3:18 [illegible] and
stayed at King's Head.

June 5, 1958
  GB to USA.

August 1, 1958
  Children to USA

August 26, 1958
  Helen died. Cable 10:30.[8]

October 2, 1958
  Marie Stopes died on October 2, 1958.

October 20, 1958
  In bed with virus. Doctor at 9. Robert for night.

October 28, 1958
  Beckett's *Endgame* 7:30. First night.

November 29, 1958
  Meet train at 10. To ballet with G and R [Georgina and Rose].

N.D. 1958
  Book. Who Cares?
  1. How?
  2. What?
  3. Where? (regions, places, geography, scenery.)
  4. It doesn't matter when.
  5. It might be anybody.
  6. Whence and wither? (and is the same as Why.)
  (My bank manager wanted to be a ballet dancer.)
  Do madness and self-preservation always go together?

April 16, 1959
  Bashie (Sebastian Barker) is 14.

May 12, 1959
  Such a lovely hot day. People in sleeveless cotton, sandals, iris, tulip, bluebells, lily of the valley in my flat. Hostas and chestnuts out in parks. Asparagus in shops. Even the first of the strawberries (a few for 3/6).

And the windows wide open, and hot winds blowing through. People sitting, smiling, basking. Babies sweating in prams.

My mind baulks at concentration – any at all. Oh dear. It slithers away. Perhaps my bad habits have gone too far. But I am so happy just being alive – fit to burst – and shopping in the sun in bare feet – sandals – loitering by W. J. Smith's, the greengrocers, choosing a luxuriant lettuce, fat healthy mushrooms, uneven pale plums, smelly English tomatoes, firm but juicy.

Blue potted hydrangeas, narcissi, poppies. Roses begin to climb real and dewy and gardeny and cheaper.

People swimming in the Serpentine.

I washed my kitchen floor twice and then put on Glo-coat. I washed my hair and dried it inside in the sun. Wandering happily around the flat admiring everything, feeling so pleased to be alone and have everything ship-shape, orderly, pretty.

The Paddington life out of the kitchen window, the Mogol Hotel, [illegible] the mews, the garage with garagy noise. Out front too much noisy traffic, but the trees so miraculously leafing, so big the leaves now I can't see the church [illegible].

People sitting in the little park-through [sic] studded with beds of bright geometrical tulips. Out on the street the yellow cab-man's cafe trolley shop with groups having tea and sandwiches.

Underneath nagging guilt about undone Slopes. But on top such a brimming happiness pouring out of me all over the flat.

A very happy day.

N.D. 1959

Beckett: breathtaking bravery all that's necessary.

OK. Instead of looking for florins dropped in the scruffy backs of chairs, why don't you think up some madly lucrative articles for the vulgar press.

Well, I'm hysterical.

Why?

Every Monday now, it seems the same.

Lunge out of it. Either way.

Some way.

Scaredy!

Looking for a loophole to arrive, the painful expenditure of thought. Wearing tearing action.

Mind blanks: Numb. Why?

I am a prisoner in England. My tax laid bare. The geography of freedom, i.e. it depends on where you live what's free.

III

THE SIXTIES

Smart's home at Westbourne Terrace became ever more popular during the sixties. The two Roberts remained, George Barker and David Wright came and went, as did poets David Gascoyne, Patrick Kavanagh, and artist Craigie Aitchison. Another artist Paddy Swift and his wife Oonagh lived in the basement of the same building. Smart juggled her family, full-time professional work, free-lance writing, and friends.

The demands of such a life cost Smart her health. She developed a serious case of hepatitis and then jaundice. In 1964, following her recovery, she joined Queen *(now* Harpers & Queen*) as a full-time copywriter. In addition, for the next two years, she contributed to it a column reviewing what she thought were the best new books coming out in England. She used her column to counter what she felt was the male establishment's refusal to give proper attention to women's books.*

The mid sixties were traumatic years for Smart. She was confronted with her first serious domestic problem: her youngest daughter Rose was experimenting with drugs, and in 1964 she became pregnant. That same year George Barker returned from Rome with his new wife Elspeth. Two years later her mother died and, as a result of a power skirmish at Queen, *Smart lost her job. She had also lost the lease on her flat.*

With the family money left to her, Smart bought a cottage in Suffolk, The Dell, which would become her retreat and retirement home. She also found what she called her 'copy-shop', a small flat in Soho, where she could do her free-lance writing. It was also during this time that Rose was imprisoned for possession of amphetamines and Smart was made legal guardian of Rose's two young children Claudia and Jane. It was the same year By Grand Central Station I Sat Down and Wept *was republished and Smart would be rediscovered. At the end of 1966 Smart claimed she had fallen out of love with George Barker.*

By the end of 1967, Smart was living full-time at The Dell caring for her

two granddaughters. She was 54 years old and as fate would have it once again
living in the country and looking after young children.

The journals for this period are day journals with appointments and
addresses. They contain numerous lists and notes for commercial writing. In
October 1961 she begins what will become her garden journals. A 1965 diary
contains a list of the composers and their works in alphabetical order. There
are sporadic entries of a trip she made to Cyprus in a 1968 journal. On the
whole, there was little time left over for reflection.

January 5, 1961

Met Deakin at [illegible] at 4 to go to Soho to show Boredom pic-
tures. Did titles. Also, block country captions finished on the spot.
Then home and trying to whip myself up to write. 'Are we more
Bored?' Innumerable interruptions by all children and 'crise de GEB'.
Hopeless. No bed till small hours. Christopher played rugger.

January 6, 1961

Bored article due for Monday. Possessions due for *Tatler*. Woke
up all aches and pains. Temperature. Plodding on trying to write.
Sholto[1] came in for a few moments.

January 7, 1961

Very ill. High temperature.

January 8, 1961

Even iller.

January 9, 1961

Tom came in at lunchtime and took away Boredom article. Rose
came in with Jake Simpson and asked if he could stay night and
Paddy and Oonagh and Henrietta came in with whisky. Henrietta
slept in Georgina's bed and Georgina slept with me. Jake in
Sutherland's room. Mike ('white hiskman') in little room. Children
dancing and Oonagh and Henrietta until 6 AM. Me still in bed with
temperature.

January 13, 1961

John McNeil came to lunch and brought us sweets. Dr Stella
Murray came late and ordered me antibiotics. Trouble getting them

from chemist. Rose sat in for P and O with Imogen. Georgina went to Soho with Oonagh, but was left there when they skipped out to QE. Paddy and Oonagh and Henrietta and David Wright came in with whisky. D Wright went home first, then Henrietta.

January 16, 1961
  Georgina off to Paris at 10 to 9 in the evening. I got out of bed and bundled up and went in taxi (feeling faintly and ghastly) to see her off with Rose. She had on a jaunty Paris hat.

January 21, 1961
  Doctor came and confirmed that I have jaundice.

March 9, 1961
  11:30 to Dr Murray. Sent home to *stay* in bed.

April 24, 1961
  Went out shopping first time at Marble Arch. GEB back from Paris.

May 29, 1961
  Go to St Mary's for blood test and X-ray. GB arrived about 5 from Rome.

December 25, 1961
  GB at Henrietta's for night but came early Christmas morning. Snow. Xmas lunch at 5 or so. GB, CB, GEB, SB, RB, me, [illegible], [illegible], [illegible].

December 27, 1961
  My birthday in bed, nevertheless cooked a duck.

January 7, 1962
  In bed. GB and GEB to QE. People back, but I slept on.

April 5, 1963
  To Berkshire with GB and CB (left SB off at Staples, RB at home). Looking for cottage.

September 10, 1963
    ES and CB in Canada.

September 20, 1963
    To see Jane.

September 21, 1963
    To Cape Cod.

October 1, 1963
    Arrive London 8:05, Willard[2] here. Slept all day.

May 21, 1964
    10:30 PM: No bars open!
    11:30 PM: Airport. Top flight 459 took off half hour late due to 'security check'. We all drove back on aeroplane bus – people standing – to the main building and a few at a time got off and pointed out their luggage. Waited in a group under the dripping shed and bundled back into the bus and the plane. Coffee, tea and two little sandwiches, one cheese, one ham. Cigarettes (in bulk offered) to buy and drinks to drink only if you pressed button which I didn't realize until we were there.

June 28, 1964
    To QE and the Rose with GEB, RB, Jeff[3] and GB and Elspeth. Archer back here.

August 29, 1964
    12:30 PM Claudia Helen Webster [crossed out] Barker born. To see Rosie 2:30. To see George 4. To [illegible] etc. GB.

July 27, 1966
    Mummy died 4:30 PM.

July 29, 1966
    Mummy's funeral St Andrew's Church, Ottawa

August 11, 1966
    Back from Canada. CB met me. Slept at Rose's.

December 19, 1966
   Up from cottage 2:42.
   Rose had second daughter 2:45 PM King's College Hospital.

July 31, 1967
   My garden: today two pale lemon spikes of gladioli with a Vogue
rose again in bloom and the lobelia looking healthy. Otherwise the
garden is dominated by poppies, marigolds, nasturtiums. The sweet
peas I planted here and there are out and OK but outshone. A late
lupin – pink and yellow – is out. Geraniums. Canary creeper. The
beargarden[4] is flowery and wild dominated by mayweed.

April 11, 1967
   Georgina phoned to say David Archer died on Sunday.

April 14, 1967
   Georgina phoned to say David didn't die.

January 1, 1968
   Alone here with Claudia and Jane.

June 4, 1968
   Motored Georgina to catch early train at Diss. George arrived
and took [illegible] away. Went to King's Leg to see Julian
Trevelyan's show. Had dinner with David Garrett. Stopped by
police on way back at 12:40 at night.

September 5, 1968
   MOT car road test done, done.

December 25, 1968
   Georgina, Christopher, Sebastian, Rose, Claudia, Jane and Tim
for Christmas dinner about 4:30 around round table.

December 29, 1968
   Slept at Jeff and Jill Bernard's. Drank at Chelsworth Pub and
lunch at Jeff and Jill Bernard's, then I came home in car. (Snow
everywhere.) C and G went to London.

March 21, 1969

Clare and CB, Julie, SB, GEB, and John here for digging drains and drive.[5]

September 27, 1969

To train in ESB's [Elspeth] car with Julie. Night at GEB's. Hetta's party for William's 65th birthday.[6]

IV

THE SEVENTIES

Smart had always intended to retire to the country, and although she could not have foreseen the circumstances that would lead her there, once at The Dell she threw herself into gardening and began to turn what she called 'an old pit shaped like Australia on the map' into 'a personal paradise, a work of art'.

By the time Rose was on her feet again, married and with her children, Smart was ready to begin writing. In February 1970, she returned to Canada, where she intended to impose isolation on herself in order to write. After visiting Maxie in Pender Harbour, she went to a cabin in Little Fort on Campbell Lake, north of Kamloops, British Columbia. But she found it difficult to write. It had been a long time since she had had time to write anything other than commercial writing. During this time, however, she worked on what would become The Assumption of the Rogues and Rascals.

At the end of March, Smart left Little Fort, spent two more weeks on the coast with Maxie, and then visited her brother Russel and his family in Ottawa. She also spent some time alone in her brother's cabin. In June she returned with her sister Jane to Vermont, where Jane had found her another cabin where she could continue to work.

Smart's difficulty in writing and the isolation she had imposed on herself are reflected in the journals of this time. There are numerous lists of plants she knew and animals she saw on her walks, and detailed lists of all the meals she ate. She began to write poems again and slowly began to find the images to express what she increasingly saw as the fleetingness of time, and the beauty and pain of the past. She began to find the form for 'The Book'.

In August 1970 Smart returned to The Dell to confront more problems with Rose. She was, however, beginning to find an audience for her work; in 1975 Popular Library brought out the first American mass paperback edition of By Grand Central Station I Sat Down and Wept. She listed the reviews it received in her journal. Encouraged, she continued to work on 'The Book'. In the meantime, Jay Landesman, an American writer and acquaintance, had *created Polytantric Press in order to publish a small manuscript of poetry by Smart titled* A Bonus. *In 1978, under a combined imprint of Jonathan Cape and Polytantric Press* The Assumption of the Rogues and Rascals *was printed. Smart won the comeback of the year award. That year BBC Radio made a highly acclaimed dramatization of* By Grand Central Station I Sat Down and Wept. *For the first time she found herself in demand for public readings and interviews. Smart now turned to a new project, her memoirs. Once again she would seek isolation, this time at The Dell. Now, however, she was beginning to feel her age and felt she had waited too long to do her serious writing. The seventies journals show the slow return of Smart to her writing.*

February 12, 1970

   Fly to Canada.

   8:53–1:45 airport.

   10:15 BOAC.

   Three hours delay due to snowstorm. Arrive Vancouver about 6 PM their time.

February 13, 1970

   At Maxie's. Slept from after lunch until next morning.

February 17, 1970

   Went to Pender Harbour. (Garden Bay to see the hospital where GES was born, and Irvine's Landing where I lived, but home gone.) Dinner and evening at Hubert Evans's.[1]

February 20, 1970

   5:30 CN train to Kamloops.

February 21, 1970

   1:45 AM arrive Kamloops, to Princess Margaret Hotel.

   Bus 7:15 to Little Fort.

   Joan Winter and Little Sam met me and took me to Campbell Lake.[2]

February 22, 1970

   At Campbell Lake. Long walk over trail and mountain to road. Half-mile lift to Campbell Lake sign. 2½ miles more.

February 23, 1970

I heard birds singing by lake.

Out of my window: tall straight tree trunks; pines (what sort – identify: lodgepole?) only breaking into feathery yellowy green tufts on top; and birch, the nearest one has a pearly pink sheen and patches of grey lichen. The farther ones look dazzling white in the sunshine and against the intense blue sky. Nearest building a little woodshed, open on one side, with four round tree holes at each corner and around the front, otherwise flat knotty planks nearly 12 inches wide. The roof slopes upward and the front is iced with a voluptuous 15-inch layer of snow that looks permanent and sparkles like genuine diamonds. Next, the next cabin with one pale pink fence nearly two-feet wide, one-foot tall. The end of the cabin is thin dark brown, natural, grooved at the corners. Off-centre, a pole supports the circular tin chimney, which goes up just higher than the top of the roof. A wooded hill beyond. Behind me the stove crackles, the kettle hums.

The table on which I write is about two feet by three and a half and covered with shiny old white? vitreous enamel. On it a small glass jug full of spruce cedar, cypress, alder, birch and other unidentifiable things and some ethereal greenish grey reindeer moss lichen. One of the cedars or cypresses is a rusty greenish gold colour, off a small 8-foot tree that was even more pure gold, by the little N-eastern lake. These cedars all have leaves that branch upward only at first, then on both sides. They branch gracefully outward alternately. The stems are a scaly rufus brown.

Yesterday I walked for miles and miles, following a trail that had been snowploughed, because anywhere else you walk, you sink down through the crusty [illegible] snow, which then goes wet and cold inside your boots, and no walking, only floundering is possible. This trail wound up and down through the woods, and then up and up until you could see a range of mountainous hills on all sides, then down and round through a clearing and down a steep thickly wooded hill. Along the trail (which had no human tracks) cat paw marks, large and small, deer marks large and small, one lot of rabbit tracks. Before I came down the steep bit I smelt a musky foxy-skunky smell, but no animals. Sometimes there were big plunge tracks sideways into the deep snow. I saw chickadees and I heard one sweet birdsong from a bird unseen. I came out into a road and turned right. The road was beginning to melt. I walked laboriously along this, between small steep mountains. There was first, at the corner where I came out, a small farmhouse. A small brown cow came galloping towards me. Was it a snakefence? I passed on my left in a valley, two or three farms, all with cattle and cars. Some cattle followed a path across the snowy field to a creek – wide, shallow, and stony. I began to despair in case I was walking in a wrong or an irrelevant direction. At one farmplace, where, higher up the road from it, in a bay, a schoolbus was parked, I went down and asked directions from a very friendly, but worn and not very bright girl. She said to continue, then cross a bridge and turn right and go 'about three miles'. I sat on a log, when I was out of sight, and smoked a cigarette, but my bladder was uncomfortably full, so I plodded on. After a time an open car came along and a young man driving it with a young Indian woman and a fair 18-month-old baby asked if I needed help, and gave me a lift. First they said to the bridge and then they said up to the road to the Campbell Lake sign. There I got out and waved them away as they turned, and waddled painfully on the two and a half miles of snow-packed road. Nearly there, I met the two oldest Winter girls, looking mythological on horseback. Today, Joan said when I met her and Walter outside their house when I got back, she had seen a dog, moose and calf by a little lake and watched them walk around. Friday or Saturday, the tracker caught two huge golden eagles in his traps. He had to shoot them because there was no way of freeing them, they are so fierce.

When I got back, after tending to the outhouse and lighting our fire, I lay down, putting my feet up high in the rafters of the upper bunk to relieve the strain of the upright position which I had been in too long on my walk. Bending was then bliss.

February 2, 1970

What are all these ridiculous statistics for? Excessive. Warming up. Oiling of the machine. Inducement to engine to start. Also, perhaps better from outside to invade than vice versa. Dreamer now keeps a superficial *mind*. Days calm, happy, dread-less. Such smells of logs burning, pine, cedar. Crackle of fire. Hum of kettle. Nice to be all contained in one small room. Bed, table, clothes, food, stove, books, writing stuff, water, wood, view, bags, boots. I get my water in two yellow plastic buckets from the creek, which bursts out of its snow cover here and there. But I have to take a big scoop to fill the second, because no matter how I try, I can't get a solitary bucket upright without losing half the water. Logs and kindling are piled outside on my little veranda, where there is also a bench for sitting and taking off boots. Joan, with four-year-old Sam, is chopping and splitting logs just outside the little lean-to shed. Walter saws the tree trunks with a buzz-saw – a noisy noise. I have hung 1½lb of butter and whey of cheese in a plastic bag, with a clothes peg, to a little colander on the veranda, because it melts to liquid, the butter, in the hot cabin, and freezes again at night.

The full moon looks straight in at me in early night. I go outside along a path dug out of the snow – two feet or more either side – to the earth's level where I also deposit my wood ashes. In front is the horses' place, with their shed. Two white or grey, one little Shetland pony, and others. In the very early morning they play, especially the little black Shetland, and a black and tan who get very excited rubbing lips and nuzzling heads. A pale white watches sadly, looking as if it feels left out. But both the nuzzlers are gelded, says Joan. She says they like salt from each other's lips. But this goes on long past limbering up time.

In the evening I walked across the snowy lake at sunset. Some four or five blackbirds were singing heartbreakingly in a group of birch trees on the far east side trr-trr-trr-wheeeeeeeee. The wooded hills rise on all sides with fabulous bits of sunset colours – mauve-grey-pink-orange-gold – and all was absolutely still and quiet except for these birds. They braced themselves and jerked their tails and bodies as they sang. But they were too high up and the light was too obscure to see any identifying marks.

February 25, 1970

Joan thinks the birds might be a very early arrival of red-winged blackbirds.

At dusk little Sam and I went to try to hear them again but it was later than yesterday, and there was no sign or sound.

Earlier, Joan, Sam and I went looking for clay along the road, with a bucket, basin, spade and trowel on a toboggan. Joan took samples of the grey clay she had got before, and also some dry crumbly fawn stuff to experiment with.

I found red four-piece leaves of *cornus canadensis*, what may be Kennekinuck (or bearberry) (*arctostaphylos, iva-ursi*) and a couple of a long trailer (*linnaea borealis?*) with tiny round leaves smaller than a dime, and another with opposing round leaves like smaller salal. Trying to identify them. All from edge of snow by drive bank.

First letter from England since I left, from GEB stating 'Dearest Mummy, alias the wanton wood-nymph'.

February 26, 1970

I walked along the little lake trail up and around to the clearing covered with tall dead mullein stalks, from where you can see mountains all around, on, round and down, to antler clearing, where it starts to go very steeply down through to dark thick forest. On the way back, a squirrel chirped from a tree or a high branch. He looked greyish, but had a rufus tail, fluffy and impertinently curled. As I walked off, he scolded me more boldly.

It's beginning to thaw. The snow on the cabin roof has shrunk to mere eiderdown size, and the snow is getting sugary. All day there's a drip from my eaves.

February 27, 1970

There is no word that means the opposite of lonely.

Walked round the lake. A squirrel scolded continuously. But I couldn't see him. A few ruby-crowned kinglets (*Corthylio calendula*) came pecking around my door at 1:45.

Went to Kamloops. About 63 miles.

February 28, 1970

The ventilator window over the sink and work top is ingenious. It's not attached, but fits. It's a length of wood nailed down. After-dinner pieces of wood shaped like this slot into them to keep it more, or less, open. A hole bored in it gives leverage.

Still reading *Walden*. Mostly marvellous, but irritating on vegetarianism and no tea or coffee etc. and chastity and sensuality being a bad thing in chapter called 'Higher Laws'. Thoreau's diet seems grossly lacking in proteins and vitamins. Not the diet for a consumptive. And he died of consumption at 45. He was 28 when he went to Walden and stayed in his cabin for two years. Finished it tonight.

March 1, 1970

A lethargic day. A waddling day. Reluctant. Unambitious. Given over entirely to reading *Portnoy's Complaint*. And trying not to eat every few minutes. Happy enough, but fattening. And, if fattening, not good enough, eh?

But this isn't sposed to be a diary so stop feeling like an accountant therein.

[Section deleted]

Ouch says the saint, as he divests himself of the love of created objects.

(Love says the hippy. Chickadee and dee dee dee deedee.)
But when he is bare and shining there,
What then? says the hen.
How now, my brown cow?
What is this;
A cool snow-locked wisdom.
Out of earshot, scream and kiss.
Calm. Dead?
A better compost
Than most?

March 3, 1970

O how sweet my cabin smells. Pine, spruce, Douglas fir, red cedar and with logs burning. And coffee and cigarettes. Shiny polished red of mahonie repons leaves.

March 4, 1970

What do I want to say? I'd better get *this* clear. 'How it feels to be me.' After wild love, universal love, [illegible] of love, *dishing* it out, everybody insatiable for it. O yes, getting it back – but . . . When is the time for action? Slashing through the slush. Everybody hurt and crying. Artist and saint. Still unsolved (by me) whether they're parallel (and can never meet) and incompatible, or . . . But I feel bad, wicked, naughty not exercising the gifts (reproachful horses in my stable). I'd take a forceful pill, if I had one. I'd try every trick. Do I try every trick? Always fighting the slothful fat wish to sink comfortably back into oblivion. A story? You know what I think of that. A moral? Ditto. Examine the past? Later perhaps. A gush about humanity? (*Lonely* Dickens.) A parade of people, so unique, and soon-to-be-gone-for-ever.

One tiny thing grasped – a packet of envelopes, the sound of a musical antique kettle, a sprig of spruce. Snowy cold extending the nose. Objects suggest. The pink paper morning infinitesimally on the papyrifera birches. Or encrusted in John Donald's jungly grey-and-white lichens. Or my totally plastic snow boots that look like seal fur and animal gut. (That's a kind, humane thing for the lords of commerce. Or can it really be cheaper than the real thing?)

Anyhow, if I babble on, this virgin notebook gets decently covered and we're both less embarrassed.

Brought in some pussy willows, still half in their shells (cases shiny polished brown, in the bursting silvery white). But only saw two spindly shrubs of them and one on my loo, and one half-way along path to lake.

The lake boomed as I was crossing it (it's been more freezing the last two or three days – very nice under the sleeping bag eiderdown – and my overcoat). It boomed dully every now and then – I thought, has something gone very wrong with their car? Is it a moose getting randy? There in the middle it boomed under me, terrifying me. There were tiny fissures in the hard snow as if someone had dragged a tiny stick along very clearly and incisively. I hurried to the reed and cattails near the shore – then watched like a brave scientist. Heard several more muted booms – but nothing to see and nothing more dramatic.

Chickadees in the distance. A hint of suspicion of a squirrel scolding.

March 9, 1970

Melancholy and despondency – is it too much of a good thing? I never did say one needs nobody *ever*. But how to arrange it so they don't take all; and that some stimulus comes from the outside without destroying everything. A deadline makes me do things. But the kind of deadline for outside which I could arrange would be for work it isn't worth doing. I don't mind that there's no market for work I want to do, but it leaves all this colossal responsibility on one. To be the cruel slave driver and the delicate instrument. Well, this *is* *the* problem. And my tricks are limited and my faith submergible. It's always been like this. I can remember days at Kingsmere when I was still a schoolgirl – despair and despondency at the blank page and trying to whip myself up and lash myself into action – settling for any kind of action – a small walk even; a learning of a few Latin names; an hour exercise on the piano. So one seems not to get anywhere at outwitting oneself. But George does. He's given a lifetime to it – with NO distraction like love and other people. Or he makes it and them a part of his plan. And anyhow nobody's methods do for anyone else. That's the forging and hacking through the wilderness that makes one's own thing of little use. Am I expecting too much of myself? I keep saying just a little, just the next simple step – plunge off for the ashtray if necessary. Shape – it's there – like the statue in the stone. Down the well – get low enough and the sweet water rewards. Is blackness agony? For it's something even *to* *want* – to bash your head against the wall to ease the pain. No pain. No wants. No life.

And still such sprightly beauty outside and all around.

Well, yesterday I took some snaps and I thought, well, how about word-snaps for a start? The film is only black and white and the camera of limited performance, but the pen is mighty and might easily catch some memorable pictures to soothe a sinking hour. But I didn't. I was too low to take this book advice. Energy, though, would have welled up to urge it on somebody else. And this social effort would have generated enough enthusiasm almost to have got me to say Hey, wait a minute! I'll do it for you.

Following a little Vaughan,[3] I ruffled through a few pages of *The Anatomy of Melancholy* looking for a useful clue.[4] Astringent, but wobbly going on the Greek and Latin [illegible]. And we're getting farther and farther from these mutually refreshing references. Origin of [illegible] attitudes. Even currently about our ancestors (small market for the interesting painstakingly well-documented book of the pioneers of Bathurst County). Only Georgina has asked about my early life. Only towards the very end of her life did I try to glean earliest memories from my mother. So every day these valuable memories are fading in the memories of the living and the living, unexcavated, are dying. But I've already said this in [illegible] but they're dying faster, in my dying memory too. Is there more to be said than that? No. But perhaps *done*.

And where are all these laughs I was looking forward to being author of? No jokes in despondency at the time. But later one is attracted to oneself and loses one's grieving despair in a ribald sociability. And they laugh, because they're too shuffled about with a self-pitying shifty despair, far from a bracing friend.

The whole world totally changes in a second. What was everything isn't anything. Back and forth. Back and forth. Catch both and the pictures begin to get dimensions. But is it worth doing? Down, it doesn't seem so. Up, it isn't necessary. Half-way up? Half-way down? (The same position, but the crux is which direction you're travelling in, isn't it?) Either way, a calm look at the landscape. Observe the emotions washing through the framework. Is it – it must be – an emotion that drives the scientist on to sit so still unemotionally observing what are said to be facts. And enough still facts, with a little geometry, can be quite a useful collection.

Of what, though? Is a fact something that really is? How absurd. A piece of birch bark really IS. In every light, the birch bark changes. In every mind it presents a different image. Feel it. Taste it. Measure it. Compare it with other birch barks. Well, what do you get? Lots and lots of lichenous information. Useful for botanists studying *genus betula*. All of it, really. But some of it he would discard: the flesh-pink flutter when the sun is going down; the slight scratchy noise when a mute breeze touches it, not so purposeful as a bird, but more secretive, more suggestive.

But an emotion is a fact too, observable from thousands and thousands of sides. Haven't you seen anger come over a face like a squall over a lake. They include storms, hurricanes, tornadoes, earthquakes in their screams. The winds are observed. Well, then?

Are the psychologists and other psychos supposed to be the scientists of the emotions? If so, they've boobed. This is not the scientific way to go about things. They should sit still, or suffer, or kick against the pricks, all the time having passionate courage to observe what goes on within. The better (more civilized) people always admit they noticed themselves doing that, feeling that, letting for instance a nasty sneaky jealousy lead them into meanness and more. Others hide and deny it.

March 24, 1970

Pale ice blue of both lakes – like cheap eggs with shells not quite formed. South side of hills mostly bare. Sugary snow still and trails and many pockets and patches that cover your boots. The robin has been here for a week – but not singing yet – only giving alarm calls. The phoebe (song is phoebe but I haven't seen it near enough to identify) sings specially in early morning.

By the little lake (or 'slew') orange cedar catkins nearly very crimson – pale ice blue lake – white snow patches, birch and poplar and Douglas fir and red cedar.

The patch of snow next to cabin now more roof than snow patch.

I've had an aversion to this book for nearly a week. An insurrection. A HATE at the idea of writing – even just plant notes.

Jangly emotion from Jane's slap-in-face letter,[5] nearly walked up to house and back for wine. Astonishment, fury, indignation, injured – but calmed myself down with cigarettes and logic.

I wish I knew definitely what that bird is that makes the plaintive two notes – pee-wee? or phoebe? – early and late (I think it's just down a semitone).

March 30, 1970

Leave Campbell Lake very early with Walter to drive to Kamloops to catch plane to Vancouver. Meet Maxie 12:45 at bus depot.

To 14 April at Robert's Creek. Staying with Maxie (Alan McIntyre from breakfast to bedtime every day).

May 11, 1970

At Bob LaRivee's cabin, Ames Hill, Vermont. Jane brought me here yesterday afternoon and she and Bob left in separate cars after a meal. I washed dishes and went to bed 8:30 and slept till 7. Today I sorted all the books (his and mine). Then I planted in the first clear bed:

Lettuce (Buttercrunch by Hawkins's seeds)
Radishes (Long White Icicle by Hawkins)
Parsley (Moss Curled by Hawkins)

Then I reorganized and arranged all the groceries and dishes. Then I had a shower and washed my clothes and hung them up outside. Then I had lunch and a rest and tea. Then I went out for a walk . . .

June 25, 1970

Essentials of life. (1) Wise. (2) Nasty. (Evidence from a dream – but a bit vague on waking.) Longing for the person from Porlock.[6] Return of the native. Dig a grave, let us bury our mothers. Places of childhood. Blue jays screaming and crying and making a squeaky noise. Smell of gas in my cabin. Hush in pine trees. Rustle in birch trees. Teapot hanging on 14-inch sawn-off tree trunk on deck veranda. Longing to avoid the painful concentration. But today 'just living' is lonely. Yesterday the old sinful unbridgeable despondency. Even with the blue blue skies. Birds so busy about their private lives but always time to be inquisitive. Answer Canada. Answer pine. A statement for the children. Well, what is there? Hysterically busy ants. Perfection, and one leans expectantly out of it; wanting it shattered? Nothing wrong, nothing to complain of. Except myself. The old restive self. The god (if there, if rich) buried so deep. Under a hard-trodden highway. Needing the suffering living: the old, old shelving of the excuse – I'll go for a walk and then I'll have a sleep, and then a cup of tea, a cigarette. Now cowardly traitor, criminal negligent, NOW. A blank. Happy or disturbed, but a blank. But today is beautiful. Butterflies large and small, all bright and erratic and gentle. Tremble of the blue jays prolonged: the other birds drawn in. (But one takes time to come to the birdtrays and samples a few sunflower seeds.) (N.B. I planted five to six sunflower seeds today.) Where's the passion? Where's the pride? What is the message? Is it useful to dip into the great cast of characters? Irrelevant, *I think*, as usual. Little green plantains. Vulgar? Vulgarly healthy? Vulgarly strong? Pretty, though, and even edible. Much scorned by mankind and especially lawn-makers. What one needs (needs? Wants. One can and must do without it) is acknowledgement of one's own sacred burden – talent, gift – to help to make it real and urgent to oneself. (Babies are there and cry and the SPCC comes and neighbours and old aunts say Fie for shame!) It *will* out if it must, say some. But it's terrible labour. Who would want it? But if it's in, it must come out. Forceps. Anything. That's the panic of childbirth – that the pain can't stop – till the child comes out. It's

in. It *has* to come out. It's the feeling (would 'agony' be too strong?).
Does it matter if this tomato plant grows up spindly and askew? It
does to the gardener. It does to me. And it should to every ME.
Supposing all the tomato plants and MEs grew askew. But that
means a purpose. Yes, but it's presumptuous to look beyond the
immediate purpose. Nosy. Just get on with the job. Yes, the job.
Get on. Something very very *small* . . .

I'm expecting visitors. Why? Just because I am. (The Person from
Porlock heard me cry.) Let me out of this. NO. I'll pin you down.
I'll cover you. I'll get you to the wall. (O but I cannot ink you at
your peril. That would be The End.)

July 1, 1970

Last night when I was in the bathroom I heard a sound like a
human sigh. Right near. Indubitably *inside* the cabin. I came into
the kitchen and looked and listened. A thud, a heavy bump from
above. Movement above the insulating tin foil. Large and ominous.
I got the broom. Thunder and trembling – suddenly from a tear
there appeared a large tail of a snake. I applied flat banging of the
broom. It lumbered out of reach. Still behind the padded silver
insulation. A big snake.

This morning half awake, inspecting my seedling boxes while
waiting for the kettle to boil, I saw a humming bird, all colours of
green, alive flashing green, whirring about the little spruce tree at
the corner of the house. It must have been a female because I
couldn't see a ruby throat.

Yesterday I walked into an old sand quarry, off the Histeawa
Trail, where a new-looking car lies thrown away in a rather ghastly
death – a pretentious car in which somebody's covetous hopes and
aspirations were once all wrapped up, and now indecently exposed
for what they were; making the heart contract, the pity, the regret,
the human shame flood in. Rusty corpses of old quarrying equip-
ment and upside-down cars were more peaceful dignified deaths,
and Mother Nature busily converting them back to elements for
new use. In the steep dug-out sand bank, rows of neat round holes,
the homes of sand martens who whirled about, giddy and gay. I
walked around, sat on a rock and smiled. Birds singing, the air full
of flying. A black hunched bird made a metallic noise and sat still

watching in a pine tree. There was a little tree-strewn pond set in reedy green. A living log came along. A beaver's head and at once a great smack of his tail in the water and he disappeared. But soon he came back and swam towards the shore with his head above water and his characteristic toothy face visible.

I skirted the swamp places and made my way back along the edge, then up through the thick spruces and hemlocks and pines with their sharp dead sticky low limbs giving me a good battering. I found no new plants, but the little wood sorrels striped, like spring beauties (claytonia) only more upright and open.

Everywhere, lately, little orange newts, looking like plastic toys.

July 15, 1970
  Liquid diet.
  Early explorers through jungle of emotions went mad. Independence drove their wits astray. (Flank off of young.) Hacking their way. Antagonizing tribes. Organizing the slave trade. Rooting up rare orchids. And where do they get to? A highway barging through. Where is the jungle? This isn't a map. It's a catastrophe. Nearly all succumbed to malaise, dysentery, instability, quarrels galore. Did any come back alive?

  Philoctetes[7] agonizing on his lonely isle. Just because he stank. Immortal because of a running sore. And all that self-pity didn't matter apparently. (Is it partly about the muse being no respecter of persons?)

  And think of the startling dispatches they sent home! Hatted and gloved ladies in Ottawa fainted at the Freudian message.

  Picture them, Freud and D H Lawrence looking up startled at each other across a [illegible] erroneous clearing. All sweaty and eager and driven by the flies. Not one of them thought of taking a Greek guide. Or even a lonely poet.

  Could they be wiping the slate clear now? Throwing the great burden of statistics overboard so that the ship won't sink? The medium is the message in a hopeless effort to reattain silence?

  'But the simple flowers, able to die unceremoniously . . .' (Pity for the watersnakes, said the ancient mariner). If I could only learn to love this book and look on it as a friend. A friend in need.
  [Section deleted]

An American robin sang this morning about 5. Once long ago when the words (all shimmering in the tenderest green) I thought O how shall I ever express such fragile beauty but even then my [illegible] puberty could also hear heartbreaking things past and time.

[Section deleted]

It's all gone. I can't remember a thing. Only these brutal roads charging through the tender woods. And a huffing puffing old man staggering up the blue/pink rocks like [illegible] but with that dragged skittishness that has given one so much for the idea of things. 'The Beauty of it! The Beauty of it!'

Beauty and pain. (Beauty and Truth.) That is all. Then what about love, eh?

You say it was only art that told us about Philoctetes on his lonely island? What about the clearing in the woods and the wiped-out pioneers and the lonely women agonizing at the too-far-off waterholes. The long meaningless care of their outdoor loos? The pain flits about the black-eyed susans and unrestrained grass and the young spruce at last intrudes into the window frames. No names. No, but what's a name. Anybody can feel these past people bursting out of the dark secretive words into this little patch of total failure. So, girls, I recommend a study of manure and the great rising and falling and fertilizing principles, which isn't sad at all, however many weep to see fair daffodils fade away so soon.

But I assume plants get pretty anxious if they can't fulfil their function. Yes, and left alone they always obey the laws. Mankind alone given leave to disobey? That seems to be the implication behind all the religions. You wanted it. You got it. Now get on with it. But millions were hard of hearing and kept wringing their empty hands and biting their useless nails. Is this supposed to give rise to pity and thereby be a help to at least a portion of the rest? And then learn to love one another?

The male cones are minute. (After *pinus retinosus*.) What the sperm-atization is to the ovum compared with the great happy [illegible] cone. They are tiny and limp and curled like discouraged worms in the boards of my rough grey table, lying abandoned with a few spent needles.

A lot goes on around what is most useful and often dishearteningly

beautiful. More so than in cities where the misery is more predomi-
nant. And can depress you so you rush to the pub for a drink. (The
man who saw the map and it gave him the will to live on his
disastrous trip in the Congo.)

How can there be so much foreboding of winter in the wind
when it is only the middle of July? The swaying trees in that angry
anthropomorphic whiny sound as if they were remembering and
dreading.

Sometimes I walk up and down and sit with my head in my hands
and look up with blank eyes in a state of pain. Then suddenly a
great sneeze, a sense of my extreme luck and wild rapture at being
alone.

But I've said all this before and much better.

However, nobody seems to have heard it, so a little reiteration of
the great flat-footed platitudes can't do any harm. A few details. A
few details, you old hermit crab. My Glad Trash Bag. Am I a glad
trash bag? Sort of.

Perhaps things are beginning or will soon. I must try to elucidate
as much as I can. Without boring myself to death. Naturally what
most people need is love dished out in great reassuring helpings.
And praise. To help them rise and be them. (One more help and
it's a hidden scream.) This I can supply.

But not while preparing this other meagre dish: bones boiled up
like a holy relic.

How sweet the trunk of the white pine smells.

My fitted sheet on the line filled out by the wind. Brings to mind
the old ships and the lift of the heart when the wind filled her sails
and she was off at last. A sense of purpose. Going somewhere. Into
the tempest. Extravagant purpose. Hopes so high. Sea so cruel. But
they knew their jobs and their muscles were hard and obedient. And
they thought I can do it! I can do it! (I can do it! cried Claudia
when I tried to help her take down her pants, aged two.) Pride
and a challenging look to observe my amazement at her new-found
accomplishment.

I can do it! I can do it! I think I'm going to be able to do it!
First inkling of a breakthrough – what bliss. The fern immediately
assumes a startling beauty and the sense of RICHNESS permeates
things all around (also the music from the radio suddenly better).
But don't *force*. Constipated or no, respect the return. (Analogy.)

(I felt a bit sick back there for a minute. I'm fasting today. I went and lay under the big pine tree. At once felt better. Put my feet up on the pine tree, after wriggling into position. All became the beautiful mitt of God.)

The body the perishable instrument – the cold, the heat, the hunger, the exhaustion, the heaviness, the difficulty of cradling it on, making it work, keeping it sweet, keeping it clean, condoning its decay. Trying not to regret its earlier phases. It's only the body. (It's only mine.) NOT to belittle it. Not to misunderstand it. Give it a chance. Urge it on when necessary.

What a darling thing to do – God – make such a flimsy vulnerable derangeable corruptible demanding delicate casing for the soul (spirit) topped off with the complicated, wildly susceptible to disturbance imprints of the mind. And washed by the fierce and uncontrollable body to frenzy, incommunicable waters of the emotions (psyche).

Wasn't it a fantastic stroke of genius on the part of the almighty to take such a foolhardy chance?

And is it proving justified? I think so.

Do the turtles fare better, go farther? No. It's the possibility of this flayed, squashable, breakable instrument – just because it's so exposed, so open, so killable, so hurtable, notwithstanding to receive a million million divergent messages so able at one and the same time while staggering on, while coping with the caring, cleaning, suffering, feeding needs. Of course great wastage leaves centuries of leaves in the forest.

Try to evoke wild gaiety. Let's have some fun and I don't mean bitter fun. Gruesome follies. No. (I don't like this pencil any more, although amazingly, it survived 35 years, and a four-year spell in a voyage trunk in a pool of water in a hostile cellar.)

Respite

Fear. Yes. (Rosie steps out into the dance with a rapt look. The Roberts greeting with a wild joy. The whistling and the grave. Christopher, aged three, leaping with rapture as the aeroplane takes off. The endless opportunities for joy that suddenly take you unawares releasing your energy like a wild bird into uncaged freedom. A bonus! (O my dear Franz. Just one more dance!) Did you get your hole? Beckett found only a dingy slit. And the breast hung down deflated and anyhow, one of them was missing.

Now I'm at the centre of the world and nothing else matters and everything is all right and a benevolence flows down over everyone and over every petty preoccupation and idiotic anxiety and irrelevant interruption and the painful paralysis is as nothing, and how can it ever have been? And soon, if I need them, I can summon the throngs of characters and the little chains of events and the immortal moments. And if they should prove to be unnecessary, then they will be concentrated like a rich epithet, but not forgotten (put me in! put me in!! calls Harry Osbourne from his thin shallow grave. Tell them H. O. was here!). I will. I will. Will you reorganize yourself into a dapper little, felicitous little adjective adoring what may seem to be merely my unnecessary egotistical unwholesome feminine woman? Or you may be reflected in the lightness and elegance of a throw-away joke. Although at eleven I may have somewhat despised your transparent social ideals, you were an artist at after-dinner speeches. And although you insulted me by giving me a lecture on manners when I was 17, I will honour you if I can. You didn't know where I was going, or what I had to do, and of course you thought your way was best, having won it with all your hard discipline and pain. I know. I know. I saw it all, even through my resentful gawking adolescent eye.

It is people like this I shall speak of and not those (and perhaps him) who made the great cataclysms. Because that was something done and accomplished, the glorious died, the triumphant bee in the orchid, that is never to be regretted, but done, done, done. Not so, these unattached (Canadian) characters flickering unfertilized and unaware by the incongruous void.

No. Or maybe no. Perhaps a polite little nonentity. (Nonentity! Fie!) (Hey, love, come here. Look, she's saying Nonentity. That's bad, and untrue.) I retract. This slight, polite character, who threw his all into being slight and polite, can perhaps lead me gently to the gorier characters waiting to destroy me on the way. My compère with hell. Beautifully groomed. Beautifully dressed, with smooth and suave white hair and small stature and well-rounded well-arranged phrases for speaking after dinner.

I am going to fast for three days. Unless somebody asks me to dinner.

But all the same, these times are gone without traces. My father,

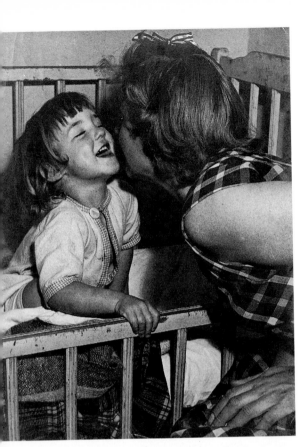

LEFT: Elizabeth with Rose, at Tilty, late 1940s

BELOW: Weekend guests at Tilty, 1951: *(standing, from left to right)* W. S. Graham, Robert Colquhoun, Robert MacBryde, George Barker with nephew John Fairfax, Paul Potts and Cedra Osborne. Elizabeth sitting in front with Rose

Rose Barker, at age
seventeen

RIGHT: Elizabeth, late 1950s

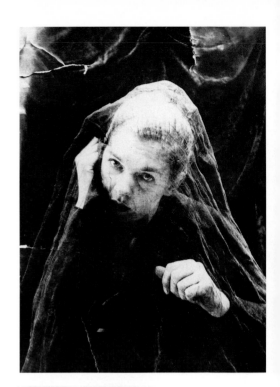

BELOW: Elizabeth writing
advertising copy, Westbourne
Terrace, early 1960s

ABOVE: Elizabeth in Canada
with her mother, early 1960s

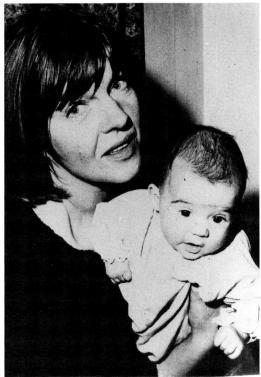

RIGHT: Elizabeth with her first
grandchild, Rose's daughter
Claudia, 1964

ABOVE: Elizabeth at The Dell with Rose's children Claudia and Jane, late 1960s

BELOW: Christmas dinner at Westbourne Terrace, late 1960s: motley collection of guests including Jill Neville, poet Brian Higgins, Robert MacBryde, George's sister Olga, Christopher and Sebastian and various other waifs and strays

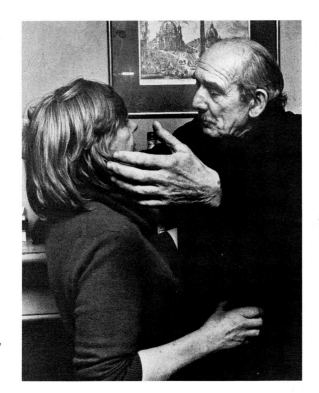

At the Dell in the early 1980s:
(RIGHT) in the garden and (BELOW)
at work

my mother, my sister, my brother and the homes and the streets
and the sounds and the ways gone without trace. And me an unbalanced lady in a flower-trimmed hat and mink cape and a blue-jeaned
young girl meandering in the sun in an unrecognizable Spark St.[8]

Somebody's hand has been at work. But I didn't see the word
behind it.

The blue hills beyond the river, still shaped the same, but not when
you get up close. The lake still untouched and sweetly breathing, the
gnarled old trees reflected around the edge, since centuries now violated. Clatter of cocktails from other verandas. Cries of kids on out-
board motors drowning the ancient cries of loons and whipperwiii.
But why should I be surprised? True. I expected that. But not the
continuous highways in and outside and around the trees – an effect
of concrete and loneliness and a total bulldozing over the old coziness,
but unknowable maybe a little nervous tittle-tattle and acceptable
back-biting and understandable refusal to gaze on ungainly horrors.
Who's helping who to see or live or bear the inescapable? No neutral
ground. No drinking ease. All to be done alone. Who's calculatedly
isolating these people lost below the pre-Cambrian shield and telling
them there's pretension(s) in a hat and gloves?

Enough of that superficial look at a Canadian city. Let time pass.
A thousand more years of pine needles dropping on the violated
forests. A million more rapes of lakes. Nobody outside the law.
Could I have misunderstood *everything*? I don't think so. It's not my
job to judge. But pity. *Yes! Pity* the *mistake.*

Is it more useful to be here than at the Dell? I think it's the absence
of all associations and the past happenings and the possibility of
present happenings. Although of course these woods evoke the
Canadian woods and cones and mushrooms and partridge berry,
Twinfloras and Self-heal and Sister's Wart are the same. Maple,
birch, pine hemlock, spruce, all around. It takes you back. But only
like arid memories in case, if memory does remain.

BGCS [*By Grand Central Station I Sat Down and Wept*] – every possible variation on that theme. Thank goodness *that*'s done. Nothing
to say *there*. The rest is more difficult and of less universal interest.
(No, I mean immediate interest. For who's been here before I have?
No one. Or do I flatter myself?)

July 16, 1970

The breakthrough is a bit bogged down. But on. On. Nibble away at the dam the dyke to block the boredom. All the same. It's the first time I've had a sneaking feeling of hope about it. Yes, it will pour. My diary will be paper enough. I've always looked after the papers. Nappies too, though I never really believed a baby would come out. The dichotomy. Where did you get your charity? Where *did* I get my charity?

Passing through degradation. (Also Humiliation.) Walking down Knightsbridge (Brompton Road?) the realization – the dark dangerous city, the wicked morbid men taking advantages, the defiling of the innocent. One a spiritual outgoing, one a diseased grabbing. Oh that thrush. The heavy heavy mindless rain. Thundery days and then that double chimey call, song, deep in the sweet green woods.

I suppose we need a drama. Well, a climax, not to say orgasm, to make an experience, a rising to a height, a subsiding. There will have to be a few humans? Snapped in action? Identifiable? But there's only me. Large as life. Pity flashes a snapshot of them caught in their dangerous surroundings. Brave and doom idiosyncratic.

Why do I think all the time of Mrs [illegible] (the neighbour who might call)? And about my daily life accordingly? And make my bed with a view to? (Examine sometime while staring into the pine Boles.)

There was a fine fast wet heavy dark rainstorm straight down and no nonsense like a long put-off pee.

The body: (see above) I'm afraid we must abuse it just a trifle if we are ever going to make a statement. Because it only wants ease and absence from shock and comfort and the strength to go on and shies off efforts that might hurt it or leave it overlooked.

But something that words can never capture: the difference between the fat circular needles of the red pine and the flat softer needles of the white pine, the shades of colour, the raindrops in them, the way they stretch soooo! Only a drawer or a painter. A person like me doesn't ever *see* them much; then suddenly! the staggering beauty and the hopeless task of communicating it.

Second day of the fast (liquids only): a very nice lighter feel. Pants looser. Limbs more movable.

A silent monologue between two middle-aged women (and the dangers I have passed!). 'Reality' quotes. Much counterpoint. Pan into details (Pagh). A few asides by very old people. And left-by-the-side people. And very young people in action. *With* music. This is going at a very pedestrian pace.

Sun out in drenched landscape.

Slapped down. Reprimanded. Told manners. Bored about. Implications of imbecility and insensitivity (mine).

All the permutations for 48 hours. (After.)

It will come. Just keep on nagging.

Sometimes it seems easier to drop.

[Section deleted]

Sometimes I want to say Shut Up to Handel with his loud insistent triumph. Could anything really be that successful and sure? It must be a lie. And a noisy one at that. Then he introduces a note of soft seduction and I am abashed and say, sorry, truly sorry, sir.

July 17, 1970

Lots more boletus in the pine woods behind the cabin. Quite a lot of blueberries ripe.

I'm a bit weak, but my mind stays pretty gymnastic. I had an egg and an orange for breakfast (but no rice cake). Chicken broth with dried milk for lunch. Walking back from the McArthurs' last night along the road palely perceptible in the dark and a nearly full moon coming up over the trees. Rising rising but not risen quite. It rose in a clear full heartbreaking way over the pines and new camp cabins across the field as the little girls were singing their Lithuanian songs and dancing. One child, with frizzy tendrils of curls out of the Renaissance was so thin and beautiful I had to restrain tears. The neck, the fine lined jaw line, the deep-dreaming expression. Thin arms and graceful body. Epitome of the youth that can't last and doesn't know what awaits it. Others with moony faces and giggles kept only comparison for adolescent problems in view. The little lost ones, holding hands, too young to leave their mothers.

N.D.

While you're doing nothing what are *they* doing (deafening roar of jets overhead).

August 1, 1970

Left Cambridge by air out to Montreal and Ottawa.

August 2, 1970

To Russel's cabin at Mont Ste Marie with Timmy and Russel and stayed night.

August 5, 1970

Arrived London 6:30 and went to Georgina's for breakfast and stayed all day with Claudia and Jane. Clare and CB came for a bit after lunch. Pub with CB, Rose, Rebecca. QE and meal with Paddy. Slept Peter St.

August 6, 1970

Brought Jane and Claudia to Dell by train.[9]

N.D.

A heavy silence with tarty intimations. It's not the skill, the craft that was thwarted but the ability to tell the truth – in the name of kindness? Humility? Humanity? Social expediency? Peace? Pah!

The greed of plants to succeed doesn't seem at all disgusting. They don't seem to need praise or encouragement or stimulation. The message is them (for them) . . .

Having screamed for distraction, I am *driven* (like a medieval malefactor) to the scary white page, still (illogically) trembling lest any look over my shoulder. When not any, no one is here and it is for that reason that I am. Driven to drivel – drivel, dribble and signs of parturition.

Special.

What is it? Glimpses, flashes in the medley, suddenly revelations to me, impossible to recall except for the absoluteness – the work revealed by lightning. Jog on in the fog. Tell the truth. Yes, but memory fails. A great protective blubber prevents knowledge to penetrate through. Hissing in the instant, only enough memory for a slight sympathy can be called up. The mind, the adolescent cocoon of all-absorbing feeling – or no feeling. And then the whorey desire to please, to entertain, to coat the nasty lethal pill . . .

Not a time to speak. What does it matter? Who listens? Who ever listens? In life people make up ways to make things possible. Sometimes I even understand (with small sharp compassion) their relationship with dogs. It's not expedient to tell the truth, for you, for them, it's important to have a working arrangement – something that gets them to their offices, their surgeries, their rehearsal halls, their notebooks, their crying night babies, their flagging lettuces, their laboratory experiments. So, you say, lies make the world go round, pads keep people functioning, the truth is best kept for Sundays, or a mere moment of . . . In poem? In vino? Would I say that? Would I say it's not necessary to fuss them? I have my own pads, blinkers, expediencies. YES but they work too well! (O speak to me speak to me, someone, and not just the sad serial of your unlovedness, your unrequited ego, your naughty lust for power.)

(If I can scribble on to the end of this book, I will allow myself the great new notebook that Sebastian gave me, that terrifies me.)

For a moment there, things eased up inside me, as if the boil would, could, might sometime somehow eventually burst and the passionate truthful poison get out into the compost heap.

The tendency to cheat – can I sternly deny it? Listen to NO ONE. Be NOT guided by their likes, scorns, prejudices, expensive superior knowledge, inferior wishes, love, hate, admonition, distaste. NO. It's like cleverly avoiding rape until you're 80 and then finding the hounds were on a different scent. The maidenhead lies dusty in the junk shop.

I had to get through.

Children.

I didn't.

They'd have been better if I'd been entirely me, with never a clever compromise, misused skill, lying gifts. Would they? This we don't know. We can't tell. Would-have-been, could-have-been. No certainty there. And certainly the world can be cruel. Would I have been sacrificing them for me, or setting them a fine example of integrity. Scorning money, showing them it doesn't matter, but how then to explain that the world is very very keen on it and even your best friends like you better for a little bit of it around, kowtow even, to the effects of fame and fortune. I did, I did only, what seemed the only, the necessary thing at the time, each time, each move.

The doubts remain, parental doubts, heavy things to carry about (did you realize *this* when you became pregnant, my dear?). How I loved you, Kewpy Good, aged four, me five. How you hated my slobbery kisses, or perhaps you were just bewildered by them? Was it your mother who made me take off the shoes on approval, and ranted at me and devastated me, with her fury, her panic about paying? 'My mother will pay for them', I said; but with my sobs and her screams, nobody heard, nobody was appeased. Then there's sex, also an ever-interesting topic. It escapes me, as an ever-boiling kettle, or lies everywhere open as a flower.

Rubadub. Itch. But not necessarily ovum fertilization. May seem to take it as a *polite* drink. Keep alive – it does that. Withered middle-aged ladies who aren't getting their share of it and lose flexibility. And they show the reverse side of ever-interesting men. Mrs Whitehouse and her lineaments of ungratified desire. Was I gratified? Therefore quietly happily evolve into seed? Drop flowers, leaves, smiling That's *that*. Or after the big event, my mother's desperate fears, warnings, hold me, keep me inactive, good little girl, perfect little lady.

Flowers aren't choosy about which bee, which bug. Come one, come all. Who, what, put around the idea that the subject should excite the art? That *that* was moral? (Especially if only the verb, the art, works.) It's often seemed as if no art were moral, to refrain from acting immoral. But then think of things, Hitler, tramplers, despoilers, wayward wanton hitters-out, squashers of gentler things, and the rest so full of passionate intensity.

Leave it, leave it.

Prufrocks to art. Hitler, to refrain.

Which brings us to omission and commission. Sins of.

NO. That's where we began. Words are so much worse than sights or sounds. True that can see can see, hear can hear, but words are naked and rude and accusing and clear enough to hurt, even the ignorant.

Hence cometh the sunset, only subject for the poem. So, it hurts me to speak. I remember the last time, far away but very sharp, the agony, the anguish, worse than birth or desperate constipation and I SHY. I balk and seek obsequiously the compensations. But they *won't do*. As this quiet time shows. Avoid, avoid. You can't.

How can Beckett be so witty in his agony? Once you start speaking, of course the agony lessens – memory of it is near, but relief makes laughter! (Here the telephone rings.)

Already tragedy turns to comedy, a better form. The leaden limp possession that is taken off one by a depression arising from a fault, a default, a non-art, a refusal to obey, a denial of the inhibited urge to speak. *Speak*, memory. Memory – is it people, places, feelings, things suffered with merriment, gaiety, excitement, expectation. The flowers flirting luminously in the gleaming can be seen or not seen – they can raise the spirits but not the dead. Do they have to be connected to something threaded to a human? If a painter saw them they might work more big magic, powerfully, but it would be not of *his* connection. The empty chair makes the window cry, etc. 'Look at nature not as in the hour of thoughtless youth' etc., etc. Why are the times depressing? Tell why, if you can.

But for 50 years I've heard people say how everything was getting worse. But what's been happening in Russia since the twenties has never happened before, the erroneous idea of the use of the common man, the hideously misunderstood idea of democracy, the mean envious misrepresentation of equality. And the aeroplanes, jets, lorries, bulldozers roaring and no place silent, no quiet craftsmen, gardeners, everything huge and commercially viable. Everybody to wear the same clothes, live in the same boxes, etc., etc.

This isn't interesting, it's long long superfluity, just a Dark Age, and everything remains the same. Or does the spark diminish? Can it go out? Barbarians have snatched the world before, and slowly slowly it revived. Survival, though, is now a favourite word. Survival, conservation, preservation.

Go back, Little Sheba, this is a diversion, a way for yourself and that for lack of a battle and truth you think you are seeking. Better to talk about old age, death even, than the sort of thing discerned in editorials. Stale and unprofitable . . . Today the sun poured down and I lay on my bed in a black mood. Butterflies lurked through the garden, and I thought I'm bored. I've seen it all before. Send me an instigator, a whipper-upper.

Does the ego lie crushed? Even that fan letter didn't raise a flutter. NO, some serious reorganization is needed to arrange cross-fertilization. It's most unnatural this hiding of needs. Look how 16 flowers shamelessly lean out to be noticed Take me! Me! Me! (But I said all this in a few words, better, long ago.) But did I make myself clear? Even this I said subsequently, long ago. Thus we go in cycles and we come again to the same place, through heavy searching, thinking, we arrive back at the same thought. (Is there another hidden, balking here? Or is it that a lurking hand tirelessly puts you back on course?) There must be millions of people writing their dramas. Young girls, of course, trying to explain their words. Politicians overwhelmed by their new importance saying: 'Today I said to the Prime Minister . . .' Union leaders saying: 'Today I said to the Unions: "Today I made history."' Alas, poor fools, no. People desperately dropping names, to be or try to be connected to great events, doers, makers, anything for a momentary illusion of immortality. Seen on TV, mentioned in Queen Victoria's letters. But inventors, good enough to be good, know that even a footnote is very hard to achieve. Some get it all unbeknownst, like the person from Porlock, Quisling, and others where names become nouns. I wonder if a pompous person would settle for that if he knew the hopelessness of his asking for more. Of course he seldom does know, and hopes against hope he's as important as he seems. Is loved. Will be remembered. Etc.

(Here, somebody came.)

January 17, 1971

Police came re: Rose in Hospital. Overdose of drugs.[10]

February 21, 1972

Georgina's son born. Sam.

October 7, 1972

Chloe Teresa Katherine born 1:50 AM. Julie and S.

August 17, 1973

Christopher and Clare getting married Caxton Hall, 10:30. Afterwards at the New Room, Tottenham Court Rd.

October 8, 1973

George, Elspeth and four children (three picked up at school) all came here for tea, dinner and night. Robert Pollet in evening. (GB and me to Bungay to get drinks.)

October 28, 1973

Joseph John Booker (Joe) born 12:15 AM. Winter time starts 3 AM.

December 27, 1973

I am 60.

Sebastian, Julie, Chloe, Rose and two dogs left after breakfast. Tea for Bookers and Christopher and me at Hase's and Michael's.[11] Christopher came back and took me to Bungay.

July 11, 1975

Trying to write 250 words about gardening for *Harper's*.

October 17, 1975

A joke.

Euphoria. Can it be induced, or is it just a lucky breeze blowing from the Elysian Fields.

Various kinds of energy.

How to break through the barrier? Memory never comes. Swing low, sweet chariot. Dip down into the sweet wastes. Piles upon piles of forgotten moments, shot through with this and that. Wild thoughts pissing in the inebriated dark. A sudden mad vision of possibilities. Caught – a glimpse of the whisking coat-tails of hope.

Sun bakes the earth. Can THEY break through that crush? A million million seeds waiting their chance. In me too? Must be. Stands to reason. But the crust is thicker. The horticulture looser and later. The gardener in the pub, pretending to be one of the boys.

But still. Come up, come up, you cagey cautious seeds, you cowardly bulbs, corn and tubers.

Avoiding the enemy, hiding in camouflage is all very well, but don't forget *for what*. Getting the precious parcel through the peril, yes, but it's the parcel that is the point.

What's in the parcel?

I've forgotten.

It's wrapped so well, stuck up with sealing wax and cellotape and stapled wires, I can't get it open.

My fingers are tender.

My strength minimal.

Always, these preliminary skirmishes.

A joke.

If I ever laughed, what made me laugh? What was the summer like, you in the Antarctic blizzard? What was the cold like, you panting in the midge-infested heat? 'Imagination's hollow dreams.'

This frail measly vulnerable changeable unmanageable instrument. Birds manage their bodies better. Look how they shake off the rain, cheerfully surveying the prospect for interesting things to eat. Where are they huddled when they're not hopping about? When it's all silent and the air is empty of their flighty forays? Sometimes so busy and thick you almost collide with them walking across the lawn. And then, nothing, each in his retreat, waiting, suffering? No, just wide-eyed for the next development.

This rain-enclosed silence is beautiful. Music from the radio, a slow hiss and spatter and drip outside, as dark as dusk, sometimes a bang of thunder, gravel-pit workings, cars in the distance, aeroplanes flying too low, tractors passing – but safe and enclosed, and thrillingly ample, so wet and uninteresting to the disrupting outside world. Private. A blessed oasis. The orange lampshade making a false but cheerful statement: *this* is the centre of the world. Books to hand. Paper and pens. Exquisite flowers open and displayed for you alone. What riches. So one says, why more? Why dig at this so ingrained, so recalcitrant mine within? Riches beyond the dreams of avarice? Or Everestly because it's there? I know this mine exists. Year after year fall layers of silt and sifting sands and rotting leaves and spattered soil and many old moth-eaten clothes. Where can the entrance be?

Joke.

Is the excavation now too hard and too late for the failing faculties that are now my trustless tools? I've kept some sharp, but even the best spade in the hands of an old hand can't move the rubbish dump. Little by little a little, but the gold lies low below. Perhaps everything's a lot easier than I suspect? I don't *suspect* it's hard, I feel I know. I know I know.

The elm has thrown a yellow arm out – the only bit of the row touched with autumn, not the highest, midway, surrounded by elmy green. All the boughs are waving and bending and everything is dripping humming with water.

There's an immanence in a certain kind of silence – in a moment (keep perfectly still) and things will be revealed – deep dreadful mysteries to shock your understanding and undermine your preconceptions. Once – in a tree – I couldn't bear the coming revelation. I ran away in terror. Was this my last chance? (Where the raspberries gathered on the moor.)

Has anything interesting evolved from knowing human beings? I can't think of anything. Comparison doesn't seem a useful thing to acquire. I felt deeply for that foolish suffering long before I knew the useless details.

The details bind one up so seeing and hearing, thinking and delving deep are shelved for puzzles.

When people are floundering in such dilemmas, is it likely they'd listen? But think of Bach, calming with his powerful vision, raising his eyes above their raging.

Or a shout.

Or a scream.

Or a secret suggestive whisper.

Look look. This is the great mystery of the world. This is the meaning of beauty and why it pierces where it touches. A rough and comradely communication is established with others known to be glimpsers: we have seen and we have understood. The costly revels are not in vain. We have hurled ourselves away for a reason that reason can recollect. Or suspect.

It's clearing. Alas. The rain abates. Bits of brightness break through the calm grey. The rumbles get remote. The menacing world comes nearer. The rumbles sound like a nearby war. Or a bomb event just out of sight. Didn't you know? O yes. Calamity occurred. The police and fire engines came, not a half mile off, while you smelled the flowers and watched the robins squabbling.

> Why did Blake say
> Sunflower weary of time?
> Every time I see them
> They seem to say
> NOW! with a clash
> of cymbals! Very
> pleased and positive
> and absolutely delighting
> in their own bright
> roundness.

I can't think of a plant that wearies of time or years.

November 3, 1975

I write when it rains. Apologies to Blake. The sunflowers are now bowing their heads in a very weary way.

I am so happy it's almost too much. A warm kitchen. A big table covered with mushrooms, books, [illegible], manual of trees and shrubs, Swinburne, Celtic Mysteries, my [illegible] Record no. 8, paper, pen, notebooks, glasses, radio, matches, cigarettes, three lots of flowers, fresh dahlias of pale pink and amethyst. A small dug-up glass jar with a poly-pody fern, a shining yellow sternbergia, a toad lily, two blue polyanthus with yellow centres, a [illegible] port jar with Korean chrysanthemums and [illegible] yellow and pink and bondros pink and bronze.

Outside the autumnal yellows, with green bits and bright red and the end of the pesky dishevelled pinks. And the slanting rain, dribbling into drains. Sometimes a slight crackle from the fire. Coffee or tea at hand, an edible at my slightest whim. And it's Monday – no duties, no expectations of interruptions, unless the coal man comes, or the peat. Yesterday it was exciting to see the Toll's nature garden, and buy on greedy sight, but more exhausting, much, especially with two trips on loaded moped, here and back with last, all more exhausting than if I had dug yards of the brambly clay on the hillock. A curious phenomenon. Even just a trip to the shop takes more of energy than two or three hours digging and replanting alone, with energy flowing in.

December 5, 1975

Your time-remembered series. But even yesterday is past in part and hard hard hard to remember. Even this morning is past and all changed changed. Is it Soho in the late 40s and 50s and early 60s that is most wanted? Cave de France? Mandrake and Gargoyle? Who I saw? What I saw? Them or me? Sights or feelings?

The heady stuff of praises and recognition sets me restless and all of a tremble. Time to squeeze out some work. Hammer a thought out into shape? Yes. Yes. Surely it will be a help? An urging on?

From now on a daily discipline. The sheer boredom of covering pages will lead to a stroke of shape, a flash of a way out. So there can be an end to this desperate want. A willing of the urge to speak, a pacification of the frustrated voice.

Radio 3 – 'An Immense Sonata Scheme' (of Liszt). Theme. Statement. Elucidation. Contrapuntal. (This and that.)

December 21, 1975
At George's with Claudia and Jane. (Rose in London.) Elspeth
and I to pub for evening drink and sat up late at home.

December 27, 1975
I am 62. Drinking John's wine with Georgina and Rose.

December 31, 1975
This Christmas: a very very long short story: a criss-crossing with
no meeting place, no love, no flowing, or even trembling emotions,
no *plan*, central meaning. Maybe we fault. Yes? Already turning my
eyes away. People. Babies. Everyone wants total attention. Explain.
Train. No. I can't. Too late. The waverer is me. Can't forge on
with a new ruthlessness after years and years of acclimatization,
mutilation, frustration, desperation.

January 5, 1976
I must think of better things to do with December and January.
They are getting me down more every year. I'll seize up if I don't
change my ways. The dread and anxiety of Christmas – this
year no climactic release – no pleasure for others, no happiness
spread about me. The garden not giving off a spark. Just
reproach and showing up my delusions about it. The children not
in a crowd. The merry spirit missing. I gave my body to be
burned, but I had not charity and it profited me nothing. Worse.
Self-hate.

February 13, 1976
Love. Children. Earning a living. Friends. Drinking. Pushed too
far, to do too much.
Silent years. Desperate frustration – desperate anxieties. So many
levels. Or one, it's a thin deep line. Straight to the point. On others
up and down to deal with distractions. What happened?
Did anything happen?
Death of friends. Old age. Gardening. Return of spring. Return
of pain. Cycle themes. To be *willing* to suffer. It's not worth writing

about the facts, is it? What did the Hepatica and the Bloodroot mean to me? Very early the daffodils.

The secret life is the real.

The poetry. The thrush in the wood.

I can't write an autobiography. No way. The drug scene? Something inhibits. The idea of one's own life. The superseding of my grandmother's by my mother's. My father's: taken over and fitted genetically into her obstreperous vision. Have I really got a fan, even one? Sometimes you catch a glimpse of someone else's idea of you – way off centre – far from where you are. Sometimes, when a child's in trouble, you tax the events, the patterns, trying to find a cause or a suggestive turning point. Why did I take our parents, our childhood, our home life so differently from Jane? What happened to her to bottle her up in the past? And to Helen, to drive her to drink and cirrhosis of the liver and death? Whenever anything is contemplated, looked at, scanned for the truth, the only report worth making is a poem. So it seemed even at the *Ottawa Journal* trying to write about women's meetings and vegetables in season.[12]

Organic matters. Gardening in the rain. Gardening in the snow. Watching plants grow. *Making* something.

Such a strange non-thing writing. Writers have to construct an importance, a sacred vocation, not to feel fiddling. Millions of demons whirl around suggestively. Cut through! Beat on regardless! If you feel foolish doing it, think of those who have done it and earned your everlasting gratitude. Beckett bringing art and gaiety to total despair. Bach sublimely soaring above the petty, the niggling and nagging, even the pain at its worst. So to go towards that – how can it be foolish? Even if you don't achieve it, the pursuit must have dignity?

Moon daisies (ox-eye); black-eyed susans (rudbeckia). Fields full of sudden surprises.

Speech, by most people, obscures thought. The clear taking in of meaning by dogs. They see what you do, they understand your real intentions. Humans can do this too, of course, if they are clarified. Even a silence over a long distance tells all, very clearly, to a concerned listener. A slight twitch or avoidance of eye, a certain intense look, or absence thereof.

Yesterday. Fifty years ago.

Stripes. Polka dots. Checks.

Stripes vertical. Stripes horizontal. Thick and thin. What am I looking for in this rubble? When trouble looms, or hysteria, noise rising to violence, shrillness disintegrating to tears, sirens warning, dogs barking, trouble about – the sensibilities freeze, the self-protective case closes down, the necessary apparatus of creation ceases. Even the openness necessary to a kind of loving is atrophied, can't respond. It would be rape to force sensuousness. They say 'I couldn't eat. It would go down in lumps.' The happy body goes into hibernation. All closes like leaves in fruit. Goes rigid and crouched like flowers in unseasonable snow, *waiting* for sunnier conditions. They have to march on blind to all irrelevancies, especially the next thing that will blow them into history.

A Mendelssohn opera is on – a lot of tiresome talking. Roly keeps scratching to come in, goes across the room standing waiting to go into the other door. Checking up on me. The day fades. Birds giving special songs. I'm cold, cold. Chilly right through. But the room is warm. The stove high. Chirruping. A blackbird?

April 27, 1976

62⅓ today.

I hear a sound like a child crying in the gusty spring wind. Or is it a saucepan coming to the boil to sterilize the cheesecloth? Forlorn wailing to tremble you back to the dangerous present. Honk from a gravel-pit machine. Dark grey clouds sailing by, casting a sprinkle of rain, and away.

May 10, 1976

I've lost the thread.

July 2, 1976

Don't try so hard. 'Take it easy, take it natural, take it slow.' Look how the moped, the Flymo respond to the gentle careless touch. Easy does it. Easy does it.

Lost words. Obscure lost words. Secret lost words. Messages. I was saying. I meant to say. What I saw, noticed, understood.

July 4, 1976

The very thin child.

O what a muddle it seems.

A short prickly muddle. The heat-wave continues, the garden is frazzled, especially the grass. Perhaps for the first time, I am bored with myself, seek a stimulant. Who? Most that come to mind offer pleasant distraction, maybe, but a repetition, a sliding into the old roles, no discovery, no cross-fertilization, no stretching. Pleasant it can be, but a polishing, a discipline for the character, for qualities of patience, love, understanding, sensitivity – not what I need, want, now. In fact they take one away from the place, the condition one wants to be in. Now – if one could get going and all flowing, then one could direct the other, proceeding along fruitful routes, once there leading to another, and begetting on all sides. What's so boring about plots? How enjoyable they are to follow in other people's work, but events, the plot of my own life makes me flag and flop with boredom. The urge rattles around inside a dried pod, noisy, desperate but unable to get out. Alien habits have hardened around it – it's safe – but dead? A small dried pea is pushed forth with a mighty painful effort and falls with a tiny clatter on the dusty floor, unnoticed.

Do I need a lover? Could be. Anonymous fly-by-night (fear of flying) or consequential? No hope of the ideal. Companionship (continuous anyhow) not wanted. But the clever little categorists miss out – no surprises, unexpected turnings, discoveries all shut out. 'After the ages', ESB [Elspeth] suggested. But the agony now is what's always been the blanks, the coming to a standstill, the impotence of the imagination. The pain to be suffered is a positive relief. Should I try to rewrite 'Dig a Grave'? NO – I was bored by it then, even with forty years' hindsight, bravery, elucidation, I can't see it cranking in my recalcitrant engine.[13]

Take down a book and play with a person – yes no. It falls flat if you're not in the mind. It's not communication I crave, and certainly not to be communicated to. You'll have to make do with what you've got.

(I kneaded a loaf. I shifted the hose. I almost deadheaded a kniphofia. I cursed the flies. They drone so. They tickle. The hot hot weather. Go to the pool. Cool. Aftermath. Sensual, unsatisfiable. Moped to Yetford. See a garden. Maybe maybe . . . OK. OK. Lassitude rules. Bitter self-hating person. Unjuicy slug. I put the bread in the oven. I scraped a bit off the beaters. I looked to see if the hose sprinkler were reaching to the right plants – my eye caught the names of Elizabeth Bowen[14] and Paul Potts (no, no, useless here, I thought, padding on) except the scraggiest example of PP makes one vow if ever so flabbily not to be *so* lazy and self-indulgent . . .

November 15, 1976

In the drought they said, 'Wash less. Let your flowers die.' I have flu or something. Weak, weepy. Bundles of plants with roots bandaged in cellophane sit on a chair outside waiting for the return of my strength. Will they die? Has it come to this, that I must choose between a thought and the life of a plant? Guilt about it gnaws away, but everything is too much. I feel helpless, hopeless, too low to call out, too weak to think. Impotent tears dribble down.

November 16, 1976

Temperature down but still not normal. Nose dribbling, but not, thank goodness, a proper cold, or worse, the suffocating agonizing sinuses. I was going to venture out to get a few of those plants in the ground, but the rain streams down and the dark encloses. All in damp drippy dark. But the weak weepy helplessness has moved or given up to more stolid desolation, glimpses of faint possibilities or effort – after all, am I not writing here?

November 17, 1976

A brisk bright day. My temperature almost normal. But my head – I mean, my thinking apparatus is muzzy, confined, and tears and helplessness lurk at the edges, where the fabric is flimsy and can give way at the slightest strain, roughness, strong current.

November 25, 1976

The gloomy season again, with the indecisiveness of Christmas paralysing the direction. Direct in a direct direction, then at least one can stagger forward as on your drunken knees to bed.

And it's at this low ebb that the rats take over, making themselves cozy in the attic. They've got plenty of purpose.

But I saw a blackbird just standing there for ages. He hardly moved his head, even, so that I wondered if he were a blackbird or just a black stone, or a misplaced stick. The first bird I ever saw looking bored and at a loose end . . .

But I've become so good at *waiting*. Patience is a sin. In me. Maybe.

Boredom. Cigarettes. Anguish. Why? Analyse. That takes strength. Holy (wholly) unattainable energy. Down the pit. Slipped too far. But that's where I want to go. Deep down, deep down. Where the gold is. Or the valuable mineral or living water. Or strange fossils? A clue? Could there be a great grieving joker down there? The shaking belly of the world. (Buddhas have bellies.)

My secret world. Did it ever have jobs? I danced sang laughed for joy. But the joke needs an [illegible], even yourself sitting outside, seeing how it would look to outsiders. Which is one step away from where I want to be. Not even in it. IT.

Today there's no music to my taste on radio. If my Mozart or Bach would back me up today.

Still, I feel a shifting. Something has budged . . .

What a long way Rose's little pill has brought me, and there might even be some nibbles in the scribbling, a starting-off place for the next crippled sorting . . .

My cigarettes are finished. Why doesn't Olive come? Now I deserve a drink. I can be calm and sociable, jolly and sympathetic. Ask questions and enjoy answers. All I needed was the little blood-letting. Such a tiny thing to ask. Such a horrible need. Why is it so terribly hard to achieve?

November 29, 1976

Looking through dusty musty old letters, notebooks. It's all there, but brought much too close. Also amazing how much I've *used* and *how*. Many notes and notebooks of George's too, a tender criticism of *By Grand Central* by him, which I had forgotten. But in my books, aside from names and diligent facts, ever-recurring depression and lethargy and blocks. A delight in clothes I'd forgotten, scrapbooks full of fashion pictures I fancied or wanted to have copied.

Then calls to Cambridge – there looking after Claudia and Rose. Rose and me to London to see a psychiatrist for her 'deep depression'.

Then calls to London and Sebastian's trouble with his eyes at Sotheby's and may not want to buy home in London if eyes prevent keeping of job and a bad weekend in Cambridge, dashing Julie's hopes. Then Claudia (12) called me to discuss Christmas.

So, other people's troubles now vibrate around in my brain lifting, shifting my own deep depression, but not improving my position, and this morning Graham Spry, nearly 77, rang from London and I shall meet him there in a day or two.

All the same, this morning I should like someone to take me out for a drink, and very reluctantly I listen to Poulenc, prepare to watch [illegible] or 'I, Claudius', or find a book, though they all look stale to me, and the garden has lost all its charm, and the gardening books their magic.

I shall go to London tomorrow, but what shall I wear? What shall I take? Today the Bank Managers wrote (kindly very quickly replying) that I could have an overdraft to see me over Christmas. So I shall take a taxi and not have to bear the elements and batter myself on the moped and not have to dread the return.

January 13, 1977

The Book has to have more shape i.e. beginning, middle and end. Statement, elaboration, elucidation, resolve.[15] Try (unless you think it would be dangerous) to make a statement about it. It's too vague just to say: Here look this is what it's like to be me, to be alive now. To have had children, to work, to try to write, to not be able to write, to try to love, sometimes to succeed, sometimes not. The conflict between work and garden, God and the ruthless muse.

What are you scared of? Boring people? Pooh. They bore you enough. Yet you still love them – oh yes. Of course. To be judged? What rubbish is this you've written?!!! 'Not one of your best efforts'. How easy though it is to be slapped down, too groggy to rise again for weeks. Abandon the idea of metre and rhyme, except as exercises to stimulate the mind.

'Work in paragraphs'. Yes. But all those paragraphs have to lead somewhere. Where does a book of poems lead? Aye, there's the rub. But that's the price you have to pay for abandoning rhyme and metre, and jerking and jotting along in so-called prose, thick-knit as it may be. To give The Book a shape, you may have to leave out some of your favourite bits; but never mind; they'll keep; they'll come in handy later. And do some boring link-up writing. Remember how boring it was linking up *Grand Central*. Yet now it's read as one, is one. Yes. I see. I'll try.

So, it begins wandering in Kensington (desolation after the war, storms, love, statement of the problem).

Learning to love stones (ancient mariner and watersnakes; explain and moss).

Learning to love people (Marble Arch, Tottenham Court Road, Soho, [illegible]).

(Can Rogues and Rascals be fitted maybe here?)

Saying I want more. Trying to write, difficulties, agonies etc. Doubts. Desperation.

Miss Smart, you are not the first. (After this: once upon a time.) Roses. Regeneration.

(Maybe better leave it not to stand on its own??)

Out of all these marvellous considerations, mind to mind, soul to soul, heart to heart, with persons known and unknown, why can I not remember a single word? Only the rich exchange, the neverto-beforgotten sympathy of closeness, the clear view into the very centre of another being lit up and totally understood. If they'd only come rolling out, they'd fill the begging pages and paste the story that's falling apart together . . .

Omission in The Book: but is it because they are unnecessary to the theme (Yes, I think), or because they touch too raw cringing words? I.e. Jane. Mummy. Russel. Sex (as people see it irrelevant here). Rose (but she's in in spots), but specifically is not needed – just the anguish of children. Gardens. Unnecessary and irrelevant. Cooking. Breadmaking (might get a glance). All these things are included in their own way, or in The Book's own way, as needed except Jane. What is for the other book, the so-called Auto-biography,[16] or long ago Canada, or something.

Goodnight. Go to sleep. Give your brain a rest. Let it sort things out through the dreamy night.

January 23, 1977

It's rather mixed up the MS – but it has to be. Logically it should be divided into my 30s and 40s then fly off into words. Instead it flew off into a storm. Also, the two crucial decades could not be only children, or even children plus only work. It has to be a sad bogged-down messy picture. Thence cometh etc. Then the decade of disasters. Disasters plus desperate gardens.

February 1, 1977
   (My Last Will and Testament; Xerox for Georgina)
   MY WILL (continued)
   I am sorry that there seems to be so little to leave after such a long life. I do hope that all the odds and ends can be divided or disposed of amicably, without cross words, injured feelings or fuss.

   I should like to be buried in a small country churchyard if this is possible (St Cross preferred).

   Each of my four children will receive a quarter of my share in my father's estate, administered by the Royal Trust of Canada, in Ottawa.

Elizabeth Smart Barker
signed 1 February, 1977

But another Will has been written this August 1982 (prepared by Laurence Scott) which says more or less the same thing, except that Rose has died, so Christopher is to receive her share to give to Claudia, Jane and James.

   E.S.[17]

ALL IS NOT WELL
   In my opinion: This water is wet, etc.
   MOZART: The heartbreaker is always in the middle – jolly emphatic analysis. (Not so Tchaikovsky.) The true laugh only after you come up from the pain, gruesomeness, panic, horror, relief! But I've said this.
   WSG [William Sydney Graham]: Not ashamed of showing us his midnight agonies and his scrubbed table, his cigarette-butt-patterned table.
   Another profound silence. In me and round about. A few chirping birds. No singing. No gravel-pit noises. A humming in my ears. Can I hear the bread rising? Strange sounds from my chest startle sometimes, until identified as such. *Scenes One Never Forgets.*
   Try not to be tempted to explain yourself, your work, your past actions. Why? Because it diminishes the pressure of speaking on paper, I think. Explain here, if necessary.
   Also, a love-point. Try not to explain others to others. Repeated as gossip, it can sound less than boring. Distorted, it is inaccurate,

though all you were looking for was guidance to their mystery. O indiscretions. But on paper truth can be ruthless. This, try not to mind. It must be. *Don't speak out loud.* It may be fun but it's not worth it. Remember how many have chattered away their talent. Lost true love in games and gossip. (O forgotten Tacitus, this is not war.)

If I were a proper novelist, endless discussion might (does) turn up interesting side-facts, facets, revealing useful aberrations, completing equations of characters.

But this is not my metier. Only inasmuch as my life or anything in my life corresponds to true things in other people's lives is it of interest, and this depends on telling the deep truths, and the surface facts are just relieving frills, a few little restful thrills, a bit of colour in the bare garden.

Could I have written about the Roberts? I'd rather keep them for my own frilly purposes than root about in the archives, even the myths, even to sharpen the record. They're not writers. Their work exists. Let them speak for themselves. If memory serves – if a point arises but not copywriting to explain them to people peering with programmes. If I get to that point in my story – but I fall off age seven, bored with sagas, scenes, the superficiality that people find as irresistible as custard creams and peanuts. Billy Joe had the exact facts so beautifully picked, the tragedy, the anguish laid so brilliantly under the black-eyed peas. It can be done, one sees. But my own way is my own way. *Now*, with such recent encouragement, with people actually reading, understanding, passive, can I not bark, or regardless, scatter my rats, and speak without cringing? We'll see.

No use waiting complacently, thinking about yourself in that sort of light. Remember how the pop stars crash and it's a rare man who comes unscathed out of adulation. *A Warning.* Yes. Even though you know that it's not you at all, you are merely a medium with a sacred duty, the lucky recipient of these electric messages flashing out onto you from the mysterious beyond. ('The great beyond'.) Would a Humanist say mystical rubbish! Probably. Let him go and do better, as George says.

But surely it was all right to look for corroboration? Yes, but attained, eschew the adulation, praise, triumph and conceit. OK, OK. Back to the drawing board.

Well, here I am. And is the corroboration a help? Or does it give me an unsettling thrill? A distraction? A sense of something done? Instead of the bleak desperation of all the awful undones?

I don't know why you're going on about this. Settle down. Settle down. Get your nose to the scent and pursue. Bend the knee and pray. Call spirits from the vast deep. Etc.

O wobbly ball! What a position the lady physician was in when we got there. A smug smile swept swiftly and imperceptibly over her face.

About parents. Shall I ever be able to write about my mother? The crunch. The painful ambiguities, dichotomies, would touch some terrible nerves – in her (after I've dared to touch mine).

Then after parents, children. This would touch fewer chords and nerves, well anyhow now, because so few live to this stage still intact and listening.

About siblings. Yes, also. The first book will be about parents and siblings. The next about children, grandchildren, great-grandchildren, etc., etc.

How could an autobiography not be about parents and siblings, anyhow, fool? The nine pages already reek of them.

Will Jane mind? Russel? (The rest live in Beechmond Cemetery now, some bones, some mere ashes.)

A passionate painful love of something or someone that you can see is full of flaws, faults, ignominies, vanity, hurt, powerlust, self-pity, self-interest, genteel brutality, waywardness, ruthlessness, selfishness, insensitivity, ego-tripping, etc.

But also a warmth, a response to revealed suffering, a vision of a passion for a seen ideal of life or a life as a picture, a talent for making occasions, a yearning towards a life as a work of art, and discipline to achieve moments such as parties, dinner-parties, dances, teas on verandas, an instant response to gaiety and flattery, [illegible] and his salad bowl, the Italian Ambassador courting sons-in-law, bunches of flowers for prudent guests.

Writing this, I can't seem to find anything to base my love on. Guilt riddles me. How she would suffer if she could read what I have written. The tears. The hysterics. She wouldn't want a true portrait of herself: but a flattering unlikeness. 'Did the psychologist think you were a nicely brought up girl?' 'How could you do this to me?' 'Clever as well as charming'.

This simple and easily satisfied vanity does, though, tear at the heartstrings. So seeable, so innocent. But some friends she had and they loved her. Did they?

What is the trembling passionate love for a mother based on? *Not* at all on her merits, character, worth. So why try to describe *her*? Only the desperate attachment that towers over your early life. Often later life too. How can I convey this? It's as vast and inescapable and omnipotent and disastrous as the weather.

Remember how she wanted *By Grand Central Station* completely destroyed and forgotten because of the things in it (very few) that she thought were about *her*, when really I was only trying to mention the severing of the bonds with parents that passionate love brings. NO portrait intended, but offence mightily, wrathfully taken.

How she used any and every weapon she could command to get her way – about George, about the book, about my movements.

Yet I went on loving her – if this is love. If what a child feels for its mother is love. If it isn't love, what is it? Later, whatever it was was joined to a passionate compassion, a protective pity that tied one in ropes, constricted movement, even thought. So strong it was that I think with guilty relief that by the time what I write about parents is published none of her contemporaries will be alive, or if alive, able to read.

Big Mumma's love, though selfish in its way, was more loyal. She was proud of the writing, the books, and didn't attempt to read, interpret, understand. She simply exulted in achievement.

I might be able to use bits of 'Dig a Grave and Let's Bury Our Mother'. [sic] Ha! (Always seeking ways out of work.) Having been a mother, one sees how one can have what one thinks is a passionate love for a child; one would certainly die for it without a moment's hesitation – kill for it – yet not *see* the child or help it to be itself, or love what it *is* – in fact, hinder it, destroy it, maim it rather than let it go. Is that the strongest feeling that there is in the world? A very blind passion. (Old Mother Nature at work here without a touch of God.)

If it weren't like that, how could the generations appear, how would the world go on? Plants do it, birds do it, rats and mice and hedgehogs do it. The only difference is *they* let them (the children) go with a realistic grace, and get on with the next thing. They push them out of the nest, migrate, hibernate, start a new brood, die, or enjoy their momentary freedom.

She achieved *a little* of the letting go late in life, after 70. But the letter about the book came when she was near 80, still distressed about her image, the unflattering light she felt it cast upon her.

Yet she was quite a bit of an artist. Her talent for hospitality was instinctive, but her discipline about the details was masterly, learned, strict – a great combination. Making homes, atmospheres, occasions appear spontaneous and no hard work, planning, organization, thought showed through the polished results.

But we're not even assessing her talents, are we? No, we're examining her as a mother, as *the* mother. We're not even interested in her as a character, are we, professor? Her childhood, her happy times in the orchard of her grandparents, sitting on the fence, eating rhubarb dipped in sugar bands.

This isn't an obituary.

She was so pleased when I mentioned happy times in the attic in an article on childhood for *House & Garden*. 'I'm so glad you have those happy memories.' Preening herself, snatching consolation, self-esteem from the nagging parental doubts.

All parents take their parenthood so *personally*. And all children take their mothers and fathers so personally too. Down into the Well, my dear, to explore these murky waters. Are they undrinkable? Can anyone wash in them?

The madonna and child. The undoubting bliss of all mothers with a newborn baby, the clean relationship all hope and warmth, and that contented semi-smile that all new babies have.

February 9, 1977

Mind split between gardening, writing, and a possible summer party. Rosie's medicine raising the spirits to happy raving pitch. Now to snatch a joke or two captured to insert in the inevitable gloom, inertia, despair. But the garden is coming alive, small bulbs are at their business, pushing through all obstacles. Possibilities also raise their hopeful heads. Passionate rejection of brown boots with black stockings – or was it vice versa? Jane and me and undies. My invoked knowledge of the rejection of her appeal to authority – shall I take her deep nearly sixty-year-old resentments and examine them one by one – fury, but rising to terror, fury, wild, uncontrollable feelings, never laid to rest. A letter to her within the text?

Worms – earth worms – the warm fellow feeling their naked vulnerability.

Eschewing anything boring (except of course the typing).

Corruption in London – a glance at the changed buildings.

The lonely decade at Kingsmere (for me: 1931–37).

If you feel love, do you need to feel power?

If you are lapped round by loving feelings, do you need to be
bossy?

Would the corruption always occur, the denial always tempt,
point a way to gain, to take advantage? The need to be important,
to be seen to be important (so may TV fare – seen and hiding in
pomposity, insisting on dignities).

Moss houses. Bush houses. Butternut tree. Old dead stump. The
pixie-mixup tree.

The staleness and the freshness. GB's repetitious evenings, con-
versations. But the delighting recurrence of refrains, choruses, the
old sayings, the old jokes, the proverbs, even Giving is Good for
You. Spring is always fresh, always a surprise, breathtaking, heart-
catching.

Moods – what are they? [illegible], manic-depressives. Anger,
euphoria, elation.

Deep down – where you have to go – can you remember the low,
the rightful low when you're soaring? In a flash, maybe, if lucky.
It's the joining of heaven and hell, the mind and the emotions, the
sight and the vision.

Things become blank again. I dissipated that pill. Used it frivol-
ously – for excitement of garden, day, anticipation. Three balls you
ride with your feet – a moment's loss of concentration and wham –
crash. Or do I have to go accumulating for even longer.

I feel lifted above all the muck that was me.

March 3, 1977

Short books. Why. Old ideas of novel. Even Jane Austen was
protesting about people who pride themselves on 'never reading
novels'.

Come out, come out whoever you are, whatever you are.

The exact circumstances seem to fascinate people. Why? A peep
into lives different from their own, clothes, homes, streets? With a
fluke of emotion they can recognize as having fleeted through them?

Always looking for the last thing.

Emotional honesty – telling the truth, looking straight in the eye the thing that hurts you.

Jealousy, envy, cowardice . . .

September 23, 1977

I don't care what form, which form. I have no ambition to *be*, only to *say*, somehow. By hook or by crook. What thunders threatens inside me. Low down, beneath the acceptable carefully tended surface.

I was here. I saw. I heard. I knew. Is that what they want I say. I also. You too?

Hello.

The to-me baffling talk about poems, content, meaning, attitudes, intentions. (Wait, reverie. It will reveal itself. Or *not*.) . . .

Is it mothers I need to speak about? (If I still cry out at night, aged 63, heard throughout the house, through several walls, still wrestling with infantile anguish, attitudes.) Bang bang. Unquiet cooker. A cough? An indigestion? I can find no reason for these alarming ragbag noises. But they distract me dreadfully. Could it have been the green coffee pot? I've moved it to the side.

It was the coffee pot and not an imminent explosion.

Aren't you ashamed?

Very. Yes, very . . .

Snapshot: the elegant body taken away in a sack, with unseemly haste.

But I hate the past. I hate yesterday.

But I still scream.

So the past is still with us, battering to get out.

An un-resolvement.

Love (i.e. George) was worked out alone, resolved to the last painful echo dying away, a metamorphosis into an impersonal, unpowering love. I never cry out in my sleep for *him*. Sometimes (when memory reruns) there's a regret, a piercing poignancy for what might have been. But no. That is done. With those ingredients, that was all that could have been made. (I did my best when I was let.)

Will my daughters ever forgive *me*?

But I forgive my mother. Alice presented me with the pity. George gave me the courage to break the surface bonds, to dare the murder-ous act of stepping resolutely into my own life. Hearing, trembling with her cries, her frantic unfair efforts to sabotage me, but going unflinchingly on.

I think I know. I think I understand. Why do I still scream, then?

Here I am in my happy Dell, with the fire going well in the Rayburn. Crocus and Beethoven pleasuring me when I look up, when I listen, a useful rain streaming down in my garden, peace achieved at last: yet after this perfect productive day, I might lie down and the screams recur.

So what is it about? Do I dare to plunge into this journey?

I fear the musty smell of the old notebooks. I don't want to lose the present. Even the photograph album with snapshots of last summer is not now. While I ruminate on them the present escapes, is swallowed!

Even if the present is just a blank, it is important. It must be given its life. But life is murder. And art is even worse. The murders of life are involuntary. Art's First Degree Wilful With Purpose Afore-thought.

So dig a grave and let us bury our mothers, but not before we've murdered her.

(My poor daughters, my poor daughters, *please* do the same for me.)

(Maybe the bits from the old notebooks – the narrative – all put in italics?)

I am escaping . . . (again and again).

Can you see a pattern now? What is it all about? It's about what Mozart's A Major Piano Concerto is about.

Birdsong. After rain. Early in the morning. The dawn chorus.

Is it boring, all this, the old facts from long ago? The saga of nursery, adolescent doubts in Acapulco? We'll see. We'll see. *But.*

All that was long ago. So I learned to love people, almost every-body. I even learned how to hate, a bit. So I forgave my mother for causing the passionate love I had for her, for casting me out of Paradise. I saw, I see, she had to. Once I was born, I was on my own. I had to be.

So why do I still cry for my mother at 63?

Mysterious and mysterious.

October 21, 1977

And it's just a load of old rubbish.

Perhaps forget it and start from bare bones as now. Whatever adheres, OK.

But still. But still, if I did use it, I could take those happy Canadian bits about my mother's charm out of 'My Lover John'.

Perhaps.

Rain swooshing, enclosing, dripping. Skies going grey, lightening, darkening.

The garden – the revelation that change is possible.

I can't start the new Honda moped.

I'm running out of cigarettes.

A Haydn quartet is on.

A steady rain spatters.

The griseline has full round drops hanging from each leaf. My eye wanders to 'Plant primulas. Move aconitum to less dry place. Weed asparagus.' Stop it. It's too diverting.

I am still alive.

Think of all those old men bashing out their memories. Patiently? Well, absorbed and interesting, thumbing through their old diaries. How about mine? Mine do bring things back with great immediacy. Is it of any interest to anyone? To me only *slightly*, like those little paintings of Canadian autumn I did – they make me remember the passion to capture it – the ecstatic appreciation of it and of the huge happiness too.

The sun has returned unexpectedly. As if the rain had never been. Except for the drops . . .

And the original passion, point, purpose comes through the early writing. It surprises me. So do the skills, the mastery. Is this long delay a pity? Or will it prove useful when I get back to the habit. When you get going you know how to snatch what you want. Yes. I always did, but the habit, as you say, was never more than squeezing bits of the day into notebooks.

Well, that's something. That comes in useful. O but how laborious, and I've used the best bits. Not necessarily, only the ones pertinent to your purpose then.

Do I want to explain myself in a cheap little obvious play, film, dialogue, story?

Well, you could try. There's nothing to stop you from branching off from there into a more interesting place and abandoning the project you first thought of.

No. You're right.

Canada. Is it worth recapturing what it was like in the 30s? For me, I mean.

Correct misunderstandings, misapprehensions. Does it matter?

Maybe not, but it was beautiful.

It's always beautiful to be young.

It's also beautiful to be old, and alive, which I am. So.

The reluctant virgin.

The suspicious daughter (an event on a boat with my father).[18]

Maxie. Alice. The Roberts. Yanko . . .

November 9, 1977

Do I want the immediacy or the distillation?

My old notebooks bring things visibly back – yet I was dissatisfied. Much that is all right is crossed out ferociously. I want to go on, somewhere else, beyond.

I don't want to lean on that young woman. What a defeat! Yet I filled those notebooks as a future help, I hoped.

Being a mother: the choppy bit.

'IF MEMORY RECUR' – *could* one stand it?

Help! Help!

Give thanks for Darwin's Berberis! (I have four, one large.) (And Christopher Smart, praise him!)

Unbalanced, unsettled, unconcentrated.

Can you lose a mastery? (On the piano, the violin, yes. But with words? thoughts? cadences?) Waiting for fusion.

Come magic synchronization.

Only advice: give everything, expect nothing, prepare, let the scene say it all.

There are honeysuckle bushes that bloom in the winter (in midwinter) and smell sweet – well what? Nothing, just a miracle. (One of millions.)

A million miracles: keep them in mind when disgust consumes.

(Forgive them for they know not what they do.)

But I was weeping, weeping all those years, scurrying through the streets harassed by deadlines. (Bitter but unbowed?)

[illegible], luminous orange and pink and red, calm yellow elms against the North sky.

All very interesting, BUT . . .

(GB says there is no such punctuation as . . .)

December 2, 1977

Mr Fristam came to say they're shooting tomorrow at 3. They'll beat the woods to the west.

One can't live too near eruptive Mania. One must get away from the trembling, the disrupting vibrations. Out of earshot of the distortions, cries, screams. Your own. Other people's. Little terrier forays in, songs, snag, seize a fiery thought out of the conflagration and back with it to place on the sacred stone, and gnaw it in peace. Is this possible? Or don fireproof armour, breathing apparatus. So far out of range, it is too still, pretty, calm, forgotten.

The hard way.

What's wrong about, what's cheating about using the old notebooks? Not necessarily anything. Provided one's judgment holds. Hard to judge though.

Snapshots. Flick through the photograph album.

Crawl up the stairs on your hands and knees to bed. Why not. Anything. Tricks, sleights of hand. Hiding the eyes. Looking. Not looking. Quick, catch it unawares.

Cold. Cold.

Tuning up the orchestra. Squeals of violins. Scrape of bass, violas. Cello revving. If you stay in the flat, you see for one the landscape. But you can't go down the well.

She's a deep one.

Twiddling with, maybe addling your brains.

So cold. What fuel that great big Rolls Royce mind needs to drive on. How many miles to the gallon to Babylon?

The violent violins, thrumming on the gut. Like calls to like. O spare me spare me the terrible tune!

'Gathering to a greatness', the bare unbearable nerve end; it vibrates, is helpless in the smell of the music, can't *but* respond.

January 8, 1978

'How badly you handle your tools, my dear, tripping over nouns, and getting entangled in adjectives and fluffing the verbs, and missing all the goals.'

January 10, 1978

If I lose myself I gain myself.

Mothers, yes, but daughters – this is harder at my age, but I see now it must be tackled. Sons too, I suppose. Responsibilities ('in dreams begin'). Who owes what to whom, or is this a fatuous, foolish idea, another pass-the-buck untenable position? Each must fight for himself, but the beauty, the civilization, the art in the heart, are the struggles in the boiling oil, who can wave a greeting message of cheer to another struggler, or sing.

Now, now comes the moment when, if necessary, I must draw myself away, use all, strength (capital), time (all that might remain), eschew compassion, consideration for others' troubles, home, garden, rumour or tumults, to rush, tread roughshod, forget irrelevancies (but who knows what might come in useful?), shut out the noise, children, cries, dogs' damage, fires going out. Lord, Lord, give me strength, ruthlessness, tenacity of purpose. Hugging it. Keeping it warm (that Spartan fat again, eating my vitals, till I am just a shell, collapsing at a breath).

Time runs out. It always does. Now or never. It always is. But death and decrepitude loom, approach, are very very near. All is not ready, far from ideal, but action action at half-cock distraction even. Pull yourself into a bullet (powder dry?), you know the target: FIRE. Sink deep. Fly high. Release yourself into scary space. Whirl yourself toward the night time end. If sudden death, all you could say is *I'm not ready, I haven't finished.* The most important bit is still unsaid. Collect your thoughts. Your Green Shield stamps will never amount to anything you really want. So spend your money and get the great desired deed done this very day. O it's like thrusting a splintered leg onto the right road. You might get there in agony but the leg can never be set back into shape. Riding on your rims, and no new tires ever to be expected.

There's a lot stored in a person of 64. How would *you* like to rifle through rooms and rooms of miscellaneous files looking for the right ones, when the house is on fire and you need to flee? Grab up the relevant and run. Canada. Early explorations. Love. Children. Work. Tilty. Gardening. Old age. Parents. Siblings. Friends.

Acquaintances. The so-called World. That meaningless word Society. Treacheries. Betrayals. Guilts. Tiny triumphs. Pleasures. Pains. Things. Hysteria. Weather. Joy, pure joy, uninvited, flying in. The imminent revelation in the pine tree. 'I could have been better. Or was it you?' Other people's useful egos. Other people's shattering everything egos. Come back, little Sheba. The Muse certainly exists. She comes. Or she won't come. She is easily insulted. Takes umbrage. Skulks. But at least she's on your side. Yes, only waiting for a proper invitation. I keep preparing the home, the table, the meal, then all gets dirty, dishevelled, undone. 'Come. No, don't come now,' I say. 'The meal is burnt, the dogs have shat on the carpet, the windows are dim, the curtains need washing and ironing, the drink's run out. Come next week. I'll try to have everything ready!'

No Muse. Our relationship must get more informal. Drop in for a chat. With Marmite, coffee, tea. There's music on Radio 3. The winter trees cast their indecipherable messages – good news if you interpret for me, Muse. I'll drop my pride and make you welcome anytime, if you'll forgive and overlook the chaos. I have been faithful to you, Erato, Polyphonia, in my own fashion.

Thalia is the one I'd like now. Are you on my visiting list, sacred lady?[19]

February 2, 1978

The stopping of the flow.

People. The murder of menstruation for so many years. Interruptions endless. From outside, but also from inside.

Cut off so often from the all-powerful energies.

The presence of people who don't *diminish you*, appreciate you diminish you to the spheres in which they operate, and only can operate, and this can be so overwhelmingly poverty-stricken that you can be reduced to almost nothing.

O beautiful February day, a fairly roguish sun coming over the ash trees in the south, and all these portents that things are about to happen, spears, shocks, signs of movement in the squashed sodden soil, faint but certain reds in the twigs of the berberis, golden life coming into the willow, a bud swollen unnoticed, fat, waiting, on the cutleafed elder.

February 18, 1978

The hardest frost yet. Everything, every branch, every twig, even the plastic clothes line rimmed with white frost and a hoary moisture on the horizon just now (11:20), a sun breaking through the moisture, grey-white of the sky. The jack-frost patterns melting from the window, where they were immeasurable this morning. Going out to hang out the clothes, there was almost a tightness in the hair of the nostrils, the snow crust so hard it batters the ankles when you crash through.

April 22, 1978

Two months later. Nothing done. Alas. Horrors. But a good bash at the garden. Think of the seasons. Spring comes.

May 9, 1978

A beautiful May Day and Purcell playing. Blossom and green growth. It's too much. I can't watch it. It's unsettling. It hurts.

May 25, 1978

This won't do. What a waste. What a shameful shame. Take your eyes off the garden. Perfection is impossible. Even a vague control cannot be reached. But by [illegible] you can move the great frozen sea within you. Birth of a cow. Don't push too hard. Nag. Nag on.

Say, only two hours a day for the garden. That leaves 22. Only six or seven needed for sleep. Fifteen splendid hours at least. A fortune. And you're wasting it. Pining frustrated, set back by social events, drink, even hard horticultural labour, various kinds of love and compassion. Still, 15 hours a day times seven is a lot to squander, 105 hours a week. O vile.

And what's within grows harder, petrifies, becomes larger and more immovable, the birth worse.

We'll abandon the mother for the moment, shall we? Yes. A new start.

September 28, 1978

. . . It's great to feel a chemical change coming over your body, lifting and shifting the deadly weight that is so hard to move on your own.

I shouldn't have told anyone that I was writing, or going to, a book about mothers.

Why?

It takes away some of the vital pressure.

Yes, but if the pressure is so great, it paralyses? Better to be sitting in a vast blank than loosened and dispersed. No?

I wish I couldn't (sometimes) hear the idiot reviewers with their snide or irrelevant comments. How unhelpful they are. Could I refrain from reading them? Some wise people do. After GCS (Graham Spry, 1945), I didn't even see them, and if and when I did, forgot them immediately, or thought them funny. Get off my back, silly children.

Ah – when everything flows. Drink, people, yes, often. Alone, it's harder, but more blissful when it does.

One wonders about other people and how they deal with this lonely task. Sydney? Sebastian? Fay? [illegible]? George? Elaine?[20]

What about all those busy girls? Excited by the newness of the territory. Little scurries into the world for a fast clue-hunt. Back, empty, a vain hope. You *knew* that. So.

One knows. One doesn't know. Both at the same time. One holds closely something precious, not looking, not analysing. A vast accumulation, balanced, not spilling, desperately looking around for a place to put it before it bursts and disperses irrevocably. The knowing, the careful planning, the analysing, are all to do with the HOW. What – don't look. HOW – do look. Why, glance at from time to time.

Who, when, where, whence. No problem there.

Sacred burden. Is this too grandiose? I think not. One couldn't say it, any more than one could say it about having a child, yet it is so. These words are heavy for these light times.

The knuckle – rapper from the North.

Make up an enemy? Any use? This is not an intellectual.

Brandenburg powering me. No. 4, activity. So these rude noises are just rude interruptions. Playground noises of haphazard children.

Why describe, separately, the 24 cows in the field? Exercise. But that's not all. There's less boring ways.

I really know.

When I do, I mean. When not, all confidence is lost. One whirls around open to everything, listening, taking in, wondering, but coming to no conclusions. Sounds so small you have to be leaning expectantly to hear them. Such slight signals; a positive stand, a thumping opinion, and they'd be missed for ever.

The trick is to stand fast while whirling and listening, open and buffeted.

The trick.

O how lucky I am to be here on a Thursday morning in a rainy Dell, with all the hours my own, no fear of interruption, beautiful things wherever I look, everything I could possibly need – cigarettes, orange juice, warmth, trees, flowers, birds, Bach, books, papers, pen that writes, lights that turn on and off, even a typewriter that works. And a moped to dash off on if I have to.

Even a mind starting to move.

Equally irrelevant, the things they said then, the things they say now.

The difference – I thought we could be friends now. But no. Everyone is the enemy in that respect. No help. Only I can know. How can I keep forgetting this, having known it for 50 years? It's the devil saying Get me out of this! No way out.

Relax, baby. Is that good advice? Relaxation begun might lead you back into an amorphous mass of primeval mind (an ever wanting to be sinking back into the ooze).

They don't know.

The sunflower has risen above the archway and is going to flower. One, lower, has flowered, but keeps its face to the West. The new bud faces East. This struggling group of three gives me a lift. A hard coming they had of it.

It's the airy precision of the blue asters that grabs me when my eye catches them. The petal-rays are so narrow you can see through them, the stems are stiff, but gently arching. There are the large, nearly two-inch [illegible], the smaller (one inch and under) ones, primulas in violet blue and golden round centres. Both set off by a spray of pink (several pink) everlasting pea.

But why does it add up to beauty. What is beauty saith my sufferings, then?!

Here comes Brandenburg No. 3.

Sometimes I feel mute. Mother, what is life? What would *you* say?

Good advice he gave the girl in *Zen and the Art of Motorcycle Maintenance*: start with the first brick in the left-hand corner of the building (instead of the whole USA). A sweet man.

Rain slight, thin, vertical. As faint as damask in a napkin. What a beneficence.

But quality of God is camouflage indeed.

The anguish of receiving a present given with love and pride that you hate, feel belittled and humiliated by, yet love for the giver, the giving. The guilt of this guilty hate, squared together with this love. The guilt of even thinking of my mother with less than the total admiration that she would want, demand, be shattered by the absence of.

Everybody had a mother. Flat, bald statement.

Mother! Mother!

It touches many a nerve.

Granny! Is funny. Raises a tolerant smile. Cosy. No nub to be near. Uncomplicated affection. Or a putting up with. Lion with its teeth drawn. No danger there.

Son of a bitch; Mother-fucker; worst insults.

Grandmothers escape all this. What about fathers? A loftier, vaguer concept. 'Son of a noble father!' Fathered *on*. When did you last see your father? Who was your father? Father who art in heaven. Father forgive them for they know not what they do.

No. The mother is messy, living, terrible, excruciating reality. Known or unknown. The idea. The one having been *ONE*, welded together. The revenge of the womb. That hopeless never-again-to-be state of well-being. Cast-out cast-out cast-out.

Umbilical. The cord is cut.

Is this brutal rejection ever forgiven?

Secret intelligence.

'Useful information tied to their legs.'

This is a beautiful, *un*wasted day. Even if no apparent progress is made, every second was full of beautiful things, savoured, seen. I was alive. After a muzzy start – I can see clearly now.

Any point now, any minute now might be take-off point. Even the aeroplanes rev and run and rev again ahead then the low soar the angle of flight towards up.

When every object gives back something and recharges you,

instead of saying Bark, Fido! – same old thing used-up flat recurring sights. All new, supercharged with meaning, breath-catching, rich.

Two beans, like bugs, polished purple, sit on the undertable, with strong shadows from the lamp, emphasizing their importance.

Strange things step out of my head. Goethe appears, and weeping Werther, for instance. Some linger round. Some I send back. They hover like obsequious servants. Do you need me? No? Sorry to interrupt. Withdraw, no offence taken.

Music less than great – good, maybe – but I turned it off. It distracted without instigating. I thought: I'll listen to silence for a bit.

Not a sound. Not a bird. Then two very low, very short chirps.

But the blood pounds in my ear. My physical brain feels bursting. The smoke from cigarettes curls around here slowly.

I look around.

So this is life.

Am I expecting something?

Almost windless. Only a slight sway from the young Madeira broom. Very vertical new shoots of the garrya are absolutely immobile. Stalks of seed-podded *digitalis lutea* shoot out at an angle, and hold it like well-disciplined dancers.

It is beautiful, this well-charged nothingness. All is poised. My moccasined toe slips along the birch floor, making too much of a disturbance with its small shuffling noise, a little reasonable friction against the grittiness, the friendly immobile soil in the cracks. I like it, but stop it. I move stealthily. Breathe in the cigarette as if in a sick room. Not to disturb. Put down pen with plop. Drink coffee with slurping sound. Listening, looking, waiting. *Drinking it all in.* Finish coffee before too cold. Better when almost too hot. The cup put down makes a ringing sound on wooden table, although paper intervenes between.

These things seem unending at the time, but *are* the components of the moment. They will bring it back, if wanted, if liked.

This is happiness!

Is it better or worse than a Joke? A joke implies pain. Pain overruled, wrestled with. God come out on top of the forces of darkness. (I'm using 'the forces of darkness' in its conventional cliché connection – to think out the true meaning of such a phrase is to dive into other matters.)

A moment of completeness.

Completeness? While the unsaid nags below? Yes, well, a little pleasant non-worrying rest in the journey. A deep breath, a satisfaction. A pause in the moving.

Do I make myself plain?

I would like to give you these blue asters, this whole happy silence punctuated by short, soft musical bird-chirps; the things I can see from my 13 windows: the ring of ash tree, with very thin grey trunks and heavy dark green leaves; the frivolous festivity amazing variety of the plants (all planted by me) all around below, the leaf shapes and colours, the angles of stems, the richness of it all. And within these walls too, the objects with their shapes and colours and multifarious meanings. My fisherman's shirt hanging over the rail in front of the Rayburn to dry, helpless with dampness in arms folded whether it likes it or no. The big blue metal teapot, whose rough sides catch the light in a white bright daub. The green coffee pot, the long-loved turquoise one that I gave as a wedding present to Paddy and Oonagh (and they long ago gave me with other stuff I look after for them), all in a row on the stove, suggesting convivial gathering, people. The trays leaning together against a low shelf. The pottery bread bin that needs so much cleaning out, or makes the bread blue and mouldy. The gardening tools sitting suggestively, and the broom so often ignored. The tap leaning from the wall, but bringing back memories of filthy watering cans splashing not very directly into them to me with the brown expensive life-saving [illegible]. The typewriter leaning against the white-washed wall, each brick with a little outline of collected dust, or coal dust, or whatever it is that keeps falling from the air. Seed packets, collections of letters, mostly answered, paper, the *Radio Times*, a lined scribbler much loved for its unpretentiousness. The silent radio. Books: three red *Reader's Digest* dictionaries, *Survival Gardening* by dead Edward Hyams, *The Vegetable Garden Displayed*, *The Fruit Garden Displayed*, [illegible], W.S. Graham, Elaine Feinstein, J. Burns Singer, [illegible], Insects, Mammals, Birds. *A-Z London Atlas*, a tape recorder, a pack of cards, three dried earth stars, my glasses, their ugly case, an orange ash tray, small, round, with clean dead matches and unclean cigarette ends, a mug patterned in green trees, a few animal envelopes, an invoice for Nyssan (bulbs) Ltd., a tin of [illegible] cookies. Matches, a reassuringly full packet of Disque Bleu, with a

shiny cellophane cover. A fawn under-lampshade and an orange-red
shade, the light on, a white [illegible] going out of it over the edge,
my garden record book no. 10, just like this, but less battered, a
maroon photograph album, four red straight chairs, the seat of them
crowded with brown paper bags open, a brown Windsor-style arm-
chair with pinkish damask floral-patterned cushion and on it letters,
a cardboard box broken and overflowing, antler table with alu-
minium top, white, with black around it, and red legs and on it a
pane of glass to go in the bottom window, and putty, and tacks, and
new big white [illegible], and shears sharpener, and O all's clear.
[illegible] and a cardboard box with saved seeds, and a disreputable
tea cozy, and a little hen basket with mysterious odds and ends I
can't think what to do with, and four unripe Conference pears, and
some faithful stiff and dried-muddy garden gloves and a brown
paper bag with some unhappy looking tomatoes I bought yesterday
in the Harleston market, and under it empty milk bottles, cider
bottles waiting for home-made beer, a white bin with flour and pasta
in it, a butcher chair with the beer-making bin on it. Etc., etc.

I've listed these things, I don't know why. I haven't given them
to you. I haven't even given them to myself. In ten years, could
they bring anything back? If I'd done that sitting in Tilty, could I
remember more? The essence remains. What one always wants is
the essence. But other people like the objects. It orientates them.
Maybe. But that's nothing to do with me . . .

If I write like this every day, or only five days a week, aside
from needing several Biros a week, I'd be bound to get somewhere,
somewhere I want to be before long. I couldn't sustain the patience
of the itinerary maker. Yes, it seems so easy, like the marvellous
revelation I had about the easiness of getting rich by writing a dozen
articles all through each Saturday night, sleeping all Sunday. Why
didn't it happen? Life is not like that! Things intrude. You can't
keep Saturdays sacred. It's hard to get 12 assignments that dovetail
into each other. Each separate subject needs a long desperate travail
to itself. Anyhow, it only happened once. And the articles were for
H&G. And a load of old rubbish, even if well *put*.

Do you feel comfortable with yourself, my dear? I don't know.
Perhaps not. I am a bundle of nerves. Why a bundle? Are nerves
shaped like kindling to be tied into a bundle? A basketful of nerves?
A bowl of nerves? A drawerful of nerves?

A bunch of neuroses is all right; it has the logic of the pun. Needs bunching.

Where *does* that 'bundle' come from?

Perhaps I've stopped screaming at my mother? Just lately? But the dreams, even the afternoon dreams, get more and more primeval.

What do I mean by primeval?

We can't stop for these philosophical refinements or we'll never get anywhere. What do I mean by I, by mean, by by? What's what?

Have I loved enough? Never. But it's easy, alone and in their absence, to love people. It's their prickly presence that irritates and makes the love fly screaming. Does this mean it isn't true love? Perhaps, but one must insist on certain conditions for the extraction of words. It's only sense, like heat, of a certain strength for cooking, a knife of a certain sharpness for cutting. A spade for digging. Do not confuse the issue. Anyhow, poor Joad is dead. And even dear Pyle. The work of art is the only true tribute. Though everything contributes, every*body* contributes. The lives, the minds pile up.

Can't you see why creatures with a purpose must rush a bit roughshod by? Eyes fixed on their objective. Helter-skelter, seeing nothing to the left or right.

Is it the shape I'm looking for? I do see the shape vaguely, which means clearly enough.

I went out to get fuel for the fire and, lo and behold, *there* on top of my moped was the big carton of Nyssen bulbs at last!

A clue: order, sorting, the inexplicable pleasure of.

October 16, 1978

Energy! Please don't sulk away too long. I can't move without you.

The three sunflowers: one looks east, one looks south, one looks west.

The one that looks east looks straight at me where I sit at my table like a windless balloon.

Small sorties: a few hanging branches cut off the plum, a dead bit off the unplanted *macleaya*, deposited in the gashouse fireplace.

This is the most beautiful place in the world, to be, for me. All mine. New Zealand, the Dolomites, the Fjords, the banks of the Amazon, the Gatineaus – ah! yes. BUT. And the uncomfortableness (discomfort?) of being among strangers, in hotel rooms without books, reference books, music and so on – and the benefit of little domestic duties to break the monotony of looking, taking in, learning, reading, writing.

October 20, 1978
    What have you been doing lately?
    All is confusion. (This isn't true, exactly. All is peace. I pursue horticultural perfection. With precision and hope, although I know it cannot be completely achieved. The confusion is when you try to answer Mother what is life? Why are we here? Etc.)

October 30, 1978
    . . . How one circles round one's concerns, round and round, over and over again, sniffing at the endlessly interesting centre – What is it? Something to eat? A procreational scent luring fertilization?
    But bees go straight to the point.
    Me.
    You.
    The focus – (what?) – to focus us?
    I put on my glasses to shut out everything over 18 inches away. It is a gesture, a symbol.
    Has the passion gone flabby? I doubt it.
    Or solidified, like lava? Maybe.
    Chop, flay, hammer, pick axe. Boulders open, smooth flint is displayed.
    They want a story.
    Well, there are lots of stories, all riveting . . .

Cold.
    Slightly sickish.
    It's got to come out of *me*. *Out* of me. A birth, simply. Fertilization has long since taken place.
    One looks around, for a way out, for help, desperate, bored, urgent to give it all up, abandon it, say what the hell, to hell with it, at the same time not quit, but like a surgeon, groping distractedly for the right instrument.
    There was this person.
    There was this simple little thought.

A mushroom seems more mysterious than Cézanne's apples. Because their bodies are underground (female sexual hidden).

If one favoured one of the muses, would the other sisters be jealous?

Just because I'm old, how should I know?

A passion remains, a yes.

(Of course, I don't really believe I'm an old woman, I don't really believe I'm old, I don't even think I've lived a very long time, it doesn't feel like it. But that's by the way, and by the way, that's how everybody feels, until they can't get up the stairs, and then they say, 'O dear I'm getting old,' hoping to be contradicted.)

Worse than doomed lovers locked together in the linking parent/child relationship, starting so early when the trembling openness takes its first impressions.

(I can't! I can't! screams a little voice inside.)

Veering too near these terrible things a poison whiff suffocates, knocks out; one faints, swoons, IT'S TOO MUCH . . .

But I haven't – or have I? – gathered enough together, yet. Little bits that make the bricks. Then the bricks that make the house. (Laughter, love and kind friends – is nice, but is extra, is part of the passing.)

Stop expecting someone to come visiting.

Let the day stretch out empty, waiting, receptive.

My frilly surroundings. My surrounding frills. I need?

O garden. The love-object. So much to do. An obsession, not a release. A distraction, a diversion. Tantalization. Will-o'-the-wisp. On, lured on and on. Till you drop. And the vegetation, nothing loath to seize the chance, closes voluptuously over, smothers the little pampered darlings in a jealous grasp. 'Why didn't you love *me* best?'

A wild dash over the sandpits will put an end to this frivolity, this frittering away of a great day, a useful blue pill.

Can I see clearly now?

No . . .

A woman *is* different. There are very strong urges. Extra? Yes, I think so. I watch and listen. I am not working to preconceived ideas. I am still, blank, receptive. Yet my purpose demands a bold, forward, positive movement.

This is why it seems that a woman cannot (maybe) tangle with art (inasmuch as she is a woman and doesn't repudiate it) except in the petit-point embroidery – the environment way. And is not her true creativity (i.e. having babies) the most creative thing possible anyhow?

Yes. AND YET.

Many a woman working now would repudiate what I say. But would they UNDERSTAND what I say?

What *is* art?

Again and again this boring old mystery crops up.

I know. I've *heard* the poem. I've *felt* the WORD.

And above all, I am aware of the inconvenient gift trapped in my lap. NOT to be ignored. A sacred duty is not too strong a way to put it.

I've said all this, tightly if elliptically in *R&R*.

But it wasn't heard, perhaps.

('Writing about the difficulties of writing', one said. It wasn't that. It was about the almost impossibility of making works of art if you're a woman.)

Doesn't that sound pedestrian, horrid, bald, unmagical, arrogant? No!

Nowadays they don't even understand David Gascoyne, many of them, in spite of his brave clear truthful words, his unpolluted love of the Thing itself. Sneering and snide and blind they often are. He'd ignore them. But be hurt? I think maybe.

The push-me-pull-you on! Remember Dr Doolittle's fabulous friend.

The womb had duties, urges, necessities. Old age does too. The *spectacle* of an old woman who isn't kind, sympathetic, unselfish is painful, ugly. But separate this cozy creature from the mad, obsessed artist-monkey within, who takes the balm out of days and never rests, whose frustrations rise to shrill unheard screams as time runs out.

> Old woman, wobbling, waddling
>   Girt your crumbly loins –

See, how absurd! But, again, separate. Take the spirit, remember the skeleton, whose age is irrelevant, who is not mocked except in protective jokes, little armours for fear.

I saw the big ex-civil servant, heavy with the weight of his importance, and I saw how people really get to believe that their hush-
hush jobs, their power, their manipulation of mighty issues really is
more important than any man's struggle with god, than their simple
life on earth. The moral issue is the mighty issue, and governing,
warring, diplomatizing are only games. A house-pinned woman
thinks that avoiding dust and stocking the larder are the most important things on earth. Her job, yes. His job, too. Important in context.
But nothing compared with the real issues. The corrupting power
can be seen even in the boarding house-keeper. Power, self-esteem,
self-importance, outside adulation, it only takes one strong thought
to put them back in their place – a child crying for its mother. Jostles
in the playground.

How the lie creeps in. People give evil unfair help.

How can one avoid using the word 'God'.

Even *that* led to misunderstanding. ('A strict Presbyterian
upbringing' and other nonsense.)

November 16, 1978

Necessary, *maybe*, but not useful: miscellaneous sex en route.

Status and sex preoccupying millions. Without these they live in
a vacuum, unidentified, unalive, unhonoured. Which is a preoccupation with feeling well, happiness, contentment, etc., nothing to do
with the point, with God, art, making. If they were goods? I suppose
they could be, but very time-and-energy consuming. Distracting. So
making things little by little. So making any getting anywhere slow,
so slow, so slow.

November 30, 1978

Unruly self. Unyielding, ungrateful, unlovely self. Open, oyster!
Open, clam! Come up, mole! Be friendlier, badger. Help! Help!
Come to the boil, kettle! Rise, bread! What tunes do you hear? What
rhythms vibrate below? Why do my eggs take so long to hatch?

Baggy belly, grooved eyes, idiotic hopes. O the layers, the layers
and layers to get through, the impenetrable levels! But at least I am
not tempted by the irrelevant levels, boredom sets in, and, like
Antabuse, forbids fraternization there, lingering with intent (and
certainly the rewards wouldn't tempt me).

So? Suppose the dykes were opened (by effort unimaginable).

It would flood the wrong part of the land. It must wake up the waiting desert, the long dormant life that lies, looking dead, but not.

Remember the log cabin beyond Kamloops?

My brain connections are scrambled. Tangled wires can't point.

December 6, 1978

Abandon hope.

Sometimes I have blamed them for huddling together for warmth – scorn I've cast low. But then moments come when the silence of the solitude is excruciating and I see scorn I've cast, low. But then the moments come when the silence of the solitude is excruciating and I see that perhaps they may be right. For them, anyway. Not many *choose* to live in a stark bare place (like Alice).

February 2, 1979

Phone off. Pipes frozen. Roof leaking in three places. Too icy for moped, and anyways I have to wait in case telephone men come. In desperation, I tried the end of John's homemade wine, but it was vinegar. One sip went through me in a sharp disintegrating way, an undermining, disruptive? Corruptive? Making dissolute?

Put moped in kitchen to warm up so that I can start it. May have to push it through gravel pits to road.

February 14, 1979

Valentine's Day – a terrific blizzard and strong NE wind.

March 15, 1979

Concentrate on one point.

Blocked even to write about blockage.

Troubled shrubs.

It's a terrible place, where I want to go. You'd have to repudiate every kind of human love, especially the mother's.

I want to go there.

But this is not to say I don't need human love: various sorts are essential to survival.

How can I commit the dastardly act of going down to that dark place while soliciting the comfort for when I come back?

Nature makes mother love, parental solicitude, for the going-on of the species. Perhaps passion comes under this heading too.

God is not involved in this, any more than he is in who sleeps with who or how. Is this not clear?

What I want to explore is the severance, the necessary severance, of this wonderful completeness – in the womb, perfect, and even for many years after, a passionate connection.

No problem for the birds, off they go with never a sigh on either side.

I'm tangled up in various layers of the mother thought. From pretty and superficial to the deep ugly, murderous.

The smug mother love walking around so self-congratulatory, so sure it won't be shot at. Sacred, known to be sacred, scaring the jeerers, touching the toughies, committing acts of super-egotism under the guise of unselfishness, and with the approval of the world.

Oh but we were so cosy. We were all-in-all to each other. A total understanding.

'Mum? Mum?' I heard the young girl cry out in her sleep.

Forty years later the cry is worse, more agonized, bereft.

And the orphan's dreams? Worse. An obsessive low-lying theme. A searching hunger. A wistful wondering. A useful lack of acquaintance with the demanding facts, the unglamorous pitiable possessiveness that lies out of sight.

Is all this really troubling me? Or is it only a stage on the long way down, superficial compared with the black holes of Energy? A simple sample of the Garden of Eden? Hubris, wanting to walk and talk with God, instead of getting on with the gardening?

Collapsed in on themselves (but is collapsed the word?) and condensed to a millionth fraction of their former selves. But powerful powerful, drawing in with overwhelming suction, and able to give out HOLY energy?

And before that and before that and before that?

I'm glad this year that I had the motorway experience,[21] the blizzard experience, a slapping back to total helplessness in the face of rude forces.

'Confidence appals.'

Then where will the energy come from, the confidence to step, see, speak. I didn't need to be told that I was growing old, weaker, frailer, huffing-and-puffinger, hopelessly unable to keep up with a ten-year-old child on the run.

I'm sorry, this year, that I had to come in contact with mean minds, ignorance, ignobility. I should have liked to have remained, or be able to go back to being 'all gloriously unprepared for the long littleness of life', and have kept on imagining intelligence, kindness, insight, wit in every travelling scholar, a noble curiosity in everyone who takes an interest in the arts. I knew this was impossible: I have catered to the world's venality and vanity since I was teenage, but my knowledge then was theoretical, and I always thought there were many dazzling exceptions. Perhaps there are. I still assume everyone knows more than I do until it's blatantly obvious that their [illegible] had a different beast in view.

This is far far from conceit. Where would I find conceit? I long to be corrected by the haughty gods. But the vandalous facts, however one mulls them over, turn out to be vandalous facts. Kicks from the ignorant cannot be confused with a knuckle-rap from the headmaster. Slow work, proving to yourself what you knew from the beginning, but didn't want to believe, in case, in case, in case –

(Now for the spiral notebook at last.)

September 29, 1979

At Hetta's. Talking with Stephen. Parsley wine in garden with him and Hetta. Poetry reading at Purcell Room, Festival Hall. GB, WSG, Gascoyne, Simpson, Pinter, Wain, Heath-Stubbs.[22]

V

THE EIGHTIES

In 1980 after reading at a Cambridge Poetry Festival, Elizabeth Smart received an invitation from the University of Alberta, to be the writer in residence. It was the year Panther Books reissued The Assumption of the Rogues and Rascals. *Five months before she was to leave for Canada, on March 20, 1982, Rose died of liver complications, the consequence of paracetemol poisoning. Four months later, she would write in her journal the simple words 'Rose Died!' Smart would never recover from the death of her youngest child and although her first instinct was to cancel the trip to Canada, she decided to go as a way of putting the past behind her.*

At the end of August she flew to Canada visiting her brother in Ottawa and Maxie in Pender Harbour before arriving in Edmonton. Although she had hoped that a new milieu would provide her with the stimulation she needed, she found Edmonton sterile and the university inhospitable. Despite her contact with students and a heavy schedule of readings, interviews, and panel discussions across Canada, Smart was increasingly lonely. She also found she couldn't write, although she tried to work on a new project she called the 'Mother Book'.

At the end of the academic year, Smart moved to Toronto. She had received a grant to work on her project. Although her life in Toronto was social and she continued to travel across Canada giving readings and interviews, she was intensely lonely, and still found it difficult to write. At the end of April 1983 she returned to The Dell, her garden, family, and friends.

Back at The Dell she continued in her efforts to write and resumed her gardening. But, though she did not mention it to anyone, Smart was ill. In February she decided it was time to visit Greece with her son Sebastian. They stayed two weeks. On March 4, 1986, in London, while visiting her son Christopher she died of a heart attack. She was buried at South Elmham beside her daughter Rose. Written on her headstone are the words non omnis moriar. *The first volume of her journals was published shortly after her death.*

The last journals show Smart's attempts to break through what she called her 'blockage'. She had abandoned her 'Mother Book', and tried to resume her memoirs.[1]

March 15, 1980

. . . I'm boring myself again. This pill seems to prefer the equable social levels. Still, it keeps my mind moving – that's something. Not blockage, mere diarrhoea.

That was nearly all ideas and very little of the magic marriage of words, which *is*, after all, what writing *is*. Ideas are one a penny, yes, but not ones I can see a faint possibility of my being able to use.

'She never looks up from the garden to [illegible] the greater issues of the world.' What issues? War? The pursuit of power? Torture? Business? Poverty? These are emotions and in me too.

Compassion – sometimes one can't feel it, or anything. Then something opens or melts, and it comes gushing through. So, sympathy, concern, imaginative insights into other lives. They can't come too often, or they'd flow in from everywhere and destroy the person, and obscure the view of the navigator. If I keep track of this one female body (mind, soul, collection of whatnots, same as everybody) and observe faithfully and truly I'll tell all. Only a fool would call this self-absorbed, since I am trying, as much as is possible, to see what is going on, catch myself unawares and, if I listen carefully enough, I will hear what is true universal and which is surface disturbance. It's unmistakable, with true ardour.

Thus envy is something I can't describe from the inside, because I don't feel it, but can observe it in others – usually elaborately camouflaged, denied, inverted.

While jealousy I know all about, and how it co-habits with sexual passion, obsession, and how it is more worth the scientist's consideration.

The light fades, 5:45. Little gusts of wind but the snowflakes are being discouraged. A damp and sinister March day, at the very end of the great snow winter . . .

Confidence regained?

Before, I couldn't say I want to write.

Now, I feel hate circling somewhere around me out there.

Well, the answer to everything was, is always, ever shall be; become stronger. Be braver.

From 'Life on Earth' you can see how things only develop when they're desperately needed. (Compare the Tree Kangaroo who gropes rudely through the [illegible] like an old man injudiciously playing Tarzan.) Gills, legs, feathers, fur, pouches, eggs, wombs, mates even (once they only split); song, flight, diet, camouflage.

If nothing must be done, nothing *is* done. Why should it be? This I have often observed in myself as in the plants, birds, insects, fishes, survival.

But the conflict is: the body or the work, the what-is-called meaning and judgment, art, what is best for one is often what is worst for the other.

Be stronger, even so. Give a fair ration of obedience to the body, then stride out and ignore the scolding, clacking tongues, just trying to scare you, smothering you in comfort.

(I *was* an obedient daughter to my body – but I needed it to make good babies, look after them – now that's over, but old habits die hard. *Kill* them!)

Before I was 13, food, drink, sleep, sex, etc., never interfered. Back to where you were before this time-consuming body-battering emotion, unasking soul [illegible] began.

OK. Begin again. Beated and chopped with tanned antiquity, and still dependent on an inspiration descending like lightning from heaven. Sixty-five down and five to go, or a bit more, with luck.

Old age, aging, growing old, is what I must mention and the severing of the ties, the divesting oneself of the love of created objects (which doesn't necessarily mean that it might not be healthy and hygienic mentally and physically to take a young lover should fate bring one to hand). (I'm not sure about this at all, it's pride mostly, and fear of humiliation, that stops me from exploring possibilities.) It is curious though, to be ugly, fat, not seen as a rival by others who are love objects, even a has-been, though I never was a been – but 'you've had your life: move over and give us room.' 'I'm still me,' say the old folks with a timid stamp of their foot, a roguish, slightly cringing coquettishness that could be knocked over with feathers.

It was never just DEATH, but the decay creeping from within. The horror you carry within you that hits you at the first wrinkle and grows until it encompasses you all and you are just a funny old bit of papery flesh that bears no relation to the earlier you.

The physical weakness even if you're an athlete or a dancer, who's never stopped exercising, the liability to chills, the need for rest, the longer lengths taken for recovery, the pride that must go, if it had any physical basis, the knowledge that time is running out and you haven't finished your assignment.

But there are many compensations, even improvements in old age. I'll tell you about these later.

April 6, 1980
More large wayward wet flakes are falling. Imagine! More large wet drops beading the branches, and coldness still an inconvenience.

Is it *possible* there are people hearing me? There are tiny signs, but it seems too good to be true. Would this be a help? Or too much of a responsibility? O a help, I think, a help to know I was not a totally mistaken person piling up a small heap of old rubbish. It's a heady twilight thought to think that things *do* get through, *might* have.

Was the mother idea a dead-end, a mistake? Do I still scream?

This 'being interested in something besides yourself' – true, untrue, depending on which layer you're functioning on. They never say such things about music, or talk about a musician's egomania, though he might be, or a bore to know, or bumpy to meet. His obsessions are recognized and applauded early (with luck). (I am listening to some Chopin – so characteristic, so seductive – what mean things could anybody say about him – no story, no people, no places, etc., etc. No, of course, nothing silly.)

One weaves around the obstacles, gets up groggy from the knocks, knows vaguely but passionately, the shape of the life, the direction of the road, remembers all too well the pain of making, tries not to flinch, shy away.

I wasn't going to write about *MY* mother – only the passionate relationship – serving nature? – longer, longer than the most passionate sexual love – and more abused?

Some small thing.

Atwood's advice to her daughter: 'Be ruthless when necessary; tell the truth when you know it.'[2]

The interestingness of growing old. But how, even more than death, far more, people don't think that it applies to them. They'll always be young, strong and have the use of all their *faculties*.

It's not for bucks that I need to shape one more.

But at least I think I am beginning to shake off the jeering inhibitive voices, the slapper-downer. The bruises fade. The purpose arises, the ears begin to hear.

What am I waiting for? (Besides the Muse, the Energy, the last-minute panic, the certain desperate dash for the morning post.)

Windows all misty from boiling bones.

'O where's it all gone, my life,' wailed Maxie.

The spirit is alive.

It hides.

It manoeuvres.

But it is strong.

Matter is flimsy and pathetic in comparison. The spirit emerges over matter and its short vulnerable moment. (Blind Roly sniffing the air with joy, remembering young Roly leaping ecstatically for so much, so rich. Wounded Roly in the Santoline, in pain, reproachful, baffled, struck down, unbelievably.[3])

. . . A cold inhabitable April day. At that point a policeman knocked at the side door with a warrant for Rose's arrest. He and a young pretty policewoman came in the front. I let them in and gave them a cheque for £35. They didn't know what it was for, but that seemed to settle the matter all right.

It shakes you up a bit, the strong policeman's knock, the dreaded accident. You brace yourself for horrors and the adrenalin roars to prepare you . . . and then a silly fine, but the system all shook up. O Rose. Not the first time.

I'll make some tea. Soon I'll put the nearly risen bread in the oven.

Ravel is coming on, violins are warming up, preliminary chat . . .

Am I really old? Am I really going to die soon?

Can these things be?

Have I said I was here?

Did you know I loved you? and you? and you?

One does communicate with people after they are gone. Small murmured words take on their meaning, half gestures become quite clear, hidden things behind masks, masking behaviours, contrary attitudes float slowly to the surface long after graves are overgrown, ashes scattered, letters lost.

Where were the puzzles? The hardest to fathom were the meannesses, the unprovoked aggressions, the hits for no seeable reason, some cancerous gnawing within (but surely not simple irritation, boredom, frustration, O foolish disintegrated person?).

Now I lay me down to sleep . . .

Regret – mostly for the slow, too stately way of words, spoken (written they go off on their own life, find their right time, like seeds whirling, floating, snapping, busting, lying low for generations, till conditions are right – how I repeat myself but only after a long circular tour I return to the same place).

I tried too hard to cut through the gooey casing, knew it had better be oblique except at special moments, but what a long long waste of time. Necessary? It seems so, but why is not yet clear.

Poor people.

Still, there's nothing to tell, except what this breathing (still) nugget, this going-on person, this me, can tell you. What's the use of pretending you know what's going on in the other nuggets of life? (Stop it – you're announcing chastisements for people who don't understand. Obliterate them except for the large, compassionate, historical why and wherefore, etc.) Interesting puzzles, probably easier to solve than you think.

O I do dread the long painful making.

A beautiful young girl asked me, 'What was it like to be beautiful?'

Sometimes they almost ask me (except that they're so polite, so tentative to avoid offence), 'What's it like to be old?'

It was embarrassing to be beautiful.

It's comfortable to be old; it's so much more forgivable.

How delicious bread is. (I'm not even eating the new loaves, crust from last time is all.)

When you're hungry.

And sometimes instead you think, how heavenly water is.

And sometimes, when your eyes are clear, the greenness of the grass is the height of delight.

Muse – où êtes vous?

This stuff is too loose to make any bricks of. Is it any use at all? The thing is to keep the hand moving. Living with rats. With moles.

With rabbits. With large greedy birds. With whatever obliviously gobbles up your hopes. Lays waste your plans.

Is it any use to sniff around the catatonic? Would it be useful to know whence, why, wherefore about it? NO, only a way out, what to do *when*. Seek to know no more.

Children.

Scenes one never forgets. (One, two, three, four and so on, as needed.)

Confronting nothingness.

But it's not nothing.

But it is the possibility that it might be; while believing that it is not, while admitting that it might be.

What it *is*.

What it *was*.

But after the ises and wases?

What remains in the astral swirl?

Like rubbing sticks that make the fire, two words rubbing each other give off a spark, as near immortal as trivial ephemeral civilization can produce.

i.e. ART.

Art, for a little while, gives it a shape, celebrates its beauty, articulates its pain, puts its tears to use.

The hungry sheep look up
and Lo

Someone has been here before.

Is it just a slightly more elegant getting together for warmth, cattle close crowded in a field against enemies, storms, fear?

Can't you be contented to live with the Mystery?

Well, I danced. I was never so silly as to stop and say Why, then. It was enough, itself. And then you might say the great dancer lives on.

Live on? A little. Not for ever. I know. Never mind.

This old person, anyhow, is driven on regardless. And was, even when a young person. It seems to be the first duty. *The* assignment. No getting to the pearly gates without your homework done.

All right. Argued. I know. I always knew.

Is this just another roundabout procrastination? A no! no! I can't, don't make me! I'm frightened! It hurts!

It hurts? It's only a little boredom. Then comes the relief. Keep that in mind.

But there are bumpy amorphous places to map, there are elusive elderly passions to capture. So large, so loose, to form into a shape, a seeable shape, a usable analogy.

But everyone who lives gets to these places. Unless they let their eyes glaze over, they come to these bleak residues.

(Make your residence among the residues.)

> 'Grow old along with me.
> The best is yet to be'

(a lie, at least too facile).

Nag, Nag.

Snuffle round in circles.

Under the waffling, the scaffolding goes up. One hopes. Lo and behold, we can build up the walls, move in the furniture, decorate a bit, fill the larder. Maybe.

(Muse! you beast! come back!)

Keep to your own peculiar rhythms, let the rhymes lie, lie, lie. Another lie. They're not for the likes of I. They only obtrude, confuse. (It was different, in that little emergency a couple of years back – a lot of loose ends were heavy and cluttering up my consciousness.)

Funny how [illegible] and Louis MacNeice both write poems about longing for the Person from Porlock at the same time. But anybody who writes does so long for their interruptions. Why does it hurt so? Why is the absolute concentration so like a beast on your back?

Are we eating our own entrails? Is it hope of being spared before we get to the arteries/heart and the life starts seeping out for ever?

A mad pursuit, and yet a longing to be stopped. Any excuse to abandon the chase.

How is it done?

(Never mind why – why nag on about that, what is art? etc.)

HOW.

I don't feel superior to trees. I wish I knew all they know. I hope they will teach me. I contemplate them and try to learn. They are my elders and betters.

Kaleidoscope – colours, shapes move into different patterns.

Steady on, lads, steady on.

('Go easy on the butter, lads, it's forty cents a pound.')

I made notes in the storm. Seasick and all, I made notes. Now I use them (or should) to make a chain against the storm, against the seasickness.

A guidebook for travellers?

Not quite. Magic. Spells. 'From harmony, from heavenly harmony . . .'

Frolicking all around, I am. Gusts, wafts of delight occur. A white oval of snowdrops across the grass lifts my spirits suddenly, uproariously.

The old cosiness comes too, encircling one from the surrounding gloom.

Suddenly! The pipes of Pan! The cockiness! The sprightliness! They stomped their feet ([illegible] – why did that thrill so?) A memory of Greece before I knew it was?

'What I tell you three times is true.'

But I find myself repeating things I said 40 years ago, coming upon them huffing and puffing laboriously, again, again, finding them, but they were never lost.

I think I speak clearly enough.

But there is, isn't there, something new, something more to say? Yes, but the frame's the same. The seasons roll round. The birds sing as day breaks.

O how beautiful.

O how long, but how short it seems.

Tie up these teasing balloons bobbing about your head, make a big beautiful bunch – and then?

Prepare a place to put them.

Would I, could I, budge without a purpose?

Without art or god – but it takes great strength to be a hedonist, to be interested enough to find the game all absorbing.

Some people do?

You'd have to keep a tight hold of Vanity, Ego, ideas of Intellectual splendour (already touching art), insatiable curiosity, gluttonous greed, unending lust (but it *must* end), infantile ambition.

So you see, my dear, how the world nags? I do. Would you wish these things away then? I wouldn't dare. Who am I to say?

Only, I say, *not* for me, please.

What kind of passion is it that still inhabits me?

Caged, but nosing around, nudging me, saying Let me Out! I can't let you out, I, until I have a place where you may safely graze. Then you shall be my own, true, free-ranging passion of the years.

Build your yard, then, make your frame. Passion wants out.

What then, then? I won't be emptied then. Another grows, grows gets to the time of greatness, wants to get out and go too.

None of your business.

Only the business in hand.

Why am I off (or almost) the mother frame? I talked too much? I hustled myself, was hustled? It doesn't matter. It does.

Before you see the end, you can't begin. Even writing the silliest article, this was the rule. The first sentence contains the end, knows exactly the length, the ups, downs, singing centre, climaxes achieved, subsided, of course of course, the shaping spirit. I know.

Calm down. Rev up. A combination of both; the calmness holding down with firm determined hand, the revving raging to go wildcat urge.

Yes, but the place, the building. The brainwork, the paperwork, the legwork.

Type. Scissor. Paste. Start again. Begin again Milligan . . .

How wonderful that time's lies do fall off like old scales, the fashionable attitudes, equivocations, prevarications, dissemblings, deceits, snobberies, prejudices – they wither up, fly away – ALL IS EXPOSED. And it doesn't take long. (One of the big bonuses of living a bit longer than most.)

Is this enough for today? A day's work? The working of the ground, as gardeners say. Seventeen and a half pages to collect seeds from. Maybe next time, a collection in typing, a starting to fit the patchwork together, a serious dash at the whole. Filling in is nothing like as awful. Infiniteness could be vanquished then. Just plod, plod. With desperation making focus sharp.

What's bothering me is the long bit. I don't want to use it as it is, but don't know how to tackle. It's alive in another era, would be a sore (or juvenile) thumb.

April 11, 1980

Yesterday, today, it was possible to believe in spring. Things rushed out with such speed. That forgotten balminess was in the air. The birds were reassured. They sang, played, darted into nooks with feathers and bits of straw.

What happened to everybody then, eh?

It's the story of Roly's life, really, no more, no less. Does his great catastrophe put him in another category? Most dogs don't have the pain.

Gazing on one tree, one apple.

One mushroom, one flower.

One flame.

Receiving and receiving. When, then, is Judgment Day? Never for us? But the roar of Authority? That's just for the take-off.

So, would I have anything useful to say to a person, directly? Perhaps not. Silent sympathy seems the best of it. All the rest is in the minds of people, to be heard or not.

I wasn't snuffling around these matters in the early days. Trudge, trudge, in and out of the labyrinth of people's sensibilities and sorrows and mistakes. Better get in touch with heaven again.

The strong lifting arm.

The ruthless rush to grab with the prize.

The little drops – of blood?

Think of the opium poppy, wounded, scratched, oozing its white, then black blood, scraped off in tiny harvests.

Amazement, wonder breaks through, stops you in your tracks.

Stays your hand?

Slowly, slowly proceed to the next thing. Cut down the wild prickly roses little by little.

The pathos of the silver teapot.

If I could show – *explain*; what? The good, the glory, the splendour, the greatness, the beauty, the beneficence.

The essence (a tinge of vanilla here, all these words are dusty, embalming, unworthy. A bird's song never has this outworn air, is never liable to misinterpretation – provokes no malice). Keep small. Keep the perfect drop in mind.

A weak woman spoke. Now the May strength returns and mighty feats are as bagatelle. Well, perhaps.

May 1, 1980

The seductive siren garden. I've done an eight-day stint, all day long, every day except for Sunday afternoon. Ideas, plans, seethe and urge action. I go to do one small job, and dozens beckon and side-track. But it's 19 days since I did my exercises in this book. Perhaps I had better give way to this horticultural chomping at the bit and rush through the garden chores and moves – but *only* this season gives a chance to do certain things – it's now or never until September or October.

I did go out. I did too. I feel much satisfaction at results. But have no thoughts, no pressure in my head to write with.

I was dutifully prepared to write: a loud knock at door: a nice okey-doke man with huge cartons containing 155 lilies in urgent need of immediate planting – experts say they ought to be planted in autumn, as soon as they die down. But these seem fairly fresh and plump, only a bit of mould on them.

June 27, 1980

Half a year older, weaker, unfinished.
The season.
The sensibilities.
Lost and buffeted one gets.
Even in the garden.

July 17, 1980

Try again.
Fuzzy-muzzy mind.
Gross day. Mole bumping under the front lawn.
Neither thirsty.

December 2, 1980

Depression: a necessary zed? Eighteen healthy, wasted months. Hardly two words captured.

Fear.

Take an object. Any object. Describe it accurately. Try to invest it with vibrations and emotions you would have if you were observing it during an emotional experience (i.e. the woodspurge has a cup of three).

Why do the old *always* return to their childhood?

Prime the well . . .

How smarmy I am. Trying to make (or keep) people happy. In the interests of love, you might say (if you were charitable).

But *always* to say, to do the kind thing? What about stimulation? Use chastisement? What about love for the truth, accuracy, art? If they (people) are squashed, nothing can come of them . . .

The horror of Christmas here in The Dell.

Oct 8, 1981

I see, I notice that *BGCS* is about loving poetry – so how can I convey to the non-poetry loving world what it is, what it can mean, and how we need it?

So what is art, in fact?

Could I stand up and explain it to the Women's Institute?

Describing things, people, is just for exercise. For healthful flexibility. But not interesting.

The view of the lonely.

I knew, always knew that I am not a novelist, never was, never wanted to be. So why do the niggling markings of people who don't understand what I am lurk unhelpfully around, getting in the way.

Just because there's no *NAME* for it?

Just do it, and leave it. The academicians can have fun defining it.

What do the poets talk about in their poems?

Sweep away the dust.

I need, I want the prose paragraph, irrevocably inevitable.

Well then.

January 20, 1982

Cold.

Break the ice . . .

The body of the garden and over my dead body the pheasant struts, the hares gnaw, the rabbits kick up the earth, dig deep in the hill, excavate sand, smother the plants, moles add mountains . . .

When my little helper seizes the reins and canters one off and we rise over the snow-blocked, mind-blocked, mind-balked landscape ee! Hooray![4]

So many things whirling around.

I wait for the pipes to flow.

From time to time a garrulous trouble begins, goes on, and stops. The death of the year (a silence, an insecurity).

The sleep, the submission, the abandonment of the inevitable cycle. (But underneath, the bold, thrusting *bulbs*. Yes, already.)

The mother – the words – the urgency (Jung seemed to miss, to NOT include).

They say: but has he anything to say? 'My hands are cold,' 'I want my hole,' 'The grass is green,' 'The story *holds* me.'

The *mother* fades *for me*. Mother, children, leaving all your loved ones weeping on a faraway shore.

Could I even think of myself as any kind of teacher.

It would be very difficult. I feel so unwise, so unsure (except for the unshakeable vision) . . .

Adaption. (Beg instinct always, rather than aggressively to change, remove the obstacle, denounce the tyrant.) Still, I invent the spade, the hammer, the costumes. Outwit rather than fight. On, on, around the devious hazards.

If I have lost interest in personal relationships, personal loss, even too personal friendship?

No desire to exchange ideas, thoughts, feelings.

Yet wanting acknowledgement.

What do you make of that?

I still love people. Want in return, only the most general objective love, no hate, no distrust.

Hate, distrust could still hurt. Well, yes, lots of things can still hurt.

But what could amazingly please?

Only understanding – of what I wouldn't attempt to explain or elucidate. (They'll have to make the leap.)

No rage in the Temple's left, then? (Pity for the pathetic, the misunderstanding, the waste of their spirit, their wounds, their strange pride, misplaced.)

I never had a friend to confide in (or wanted one? Well, very early I recognized the impossibility of hearing me).

March 15, 1982

I suddenly see how to film *BGCS* on the principle of the videos to pop songs.

A wonderful voice reading it straight (*cut* to one and one-half hours) with all the rest visuals – with music – entirely enacted without speech and explanation – lovers, landscape, nasty FBI men, snow, etc., etc.

So simple! So daring! and with a brilliant photographer and director it would work.

March 20, 1982
Rose died!

March 25, 1982
[Rose's funeral at St Cross.]

ND
The memory of the pain makes the blockage the refusal, the fear to go, feet drag, is like panic-stricken donkey. When there's no pain it's hard to believe it's the real thing, it's too easy, one could go on for ever. But when this period (visibility great) goes, how can it be recaptured? Unbelievable luck, thinking back, that lucid eloquent rare time, when writing was pleasure.

ND
Do I want to, can I face my own pain alone now? Shock keeps horror at bay. Hands off. Distanced by mist and pride and drink and friends and necessities like food, babies, fires. The strong hostess. Discipline (hostess? hostages?) but until I do nothing can happen such as healing reality, the next thing. A new pain will arrive. Opener, more unprotected than the worst one, the last one (cocooned in shock) a flowing, a bleeding, a sweeping (a letting go?) but this must be borne alone . . .

So the pain sits still, crouching, heavy, occupying all my inside, always, all the time, whatever my outside does.

Dear God, thank you for the great gift of alcohol given to us miserable sinners in our need – a BLOW, a tremendous failure. To bring somebody into the world and not be able to explain the point of it. Great capacity for pleasure, no capacity for pain. Great strength, pride, but no knowledge of cause and effect. The morning after the night. Unprotected against 'the long bitterness of life'. The mean, the ungenerous. But why couldn't I have told her about what I knew, about her, about life – No, I stuck to my own [illegible] in an effort maybe to save myself. Ignoring for me, shame, torment, failure, a vague love is not enough. *Make actions urgent, it's nature clear!* This I failed to do. And she suffered, cried for help, and still loved on. Was bewildered and found it too painful. Died.

Where, if anywhere, do a mother's responsibilities end?

June 18, 1982

A deep desperate blank. Is it worse than positive pain? Pride is braced to bear pain. All helpers are in hiding from the blank state. Memory lies dogged. All past experience is out of earshot, unavailable. Emotions unimaginable. Appalling pall. Why? What causes it? Inexplicable curse. Could it be useful in a negative way? It seems so shameful when everything is so beautiful, when I lack nothing for perfect contentment.

What is going on inside my blocked and bottled psyche?

Why have I no thoughts, needs, desires? Is it something everybody experiences sometimes? Or just all writers sometimes, or just some writers sometimes? (Painters? Composers? Less evidence for them.)

Foxglove, dogwood, [illegible], elder blossom, blue geranium, Siberian iris. So amazing but ineffectual. Even Hypolyte, Gypsy Boy, Fantin-Latour – old roses with charm and scent. Even Alberti emerging exuberantly and the perennial pea rising triumphantly. Birds singing, chirping. A rain just stopped.

'I may not hope for outward form to miss', etc. Always this lesson recurs. Fifty years hasn't slapped down that kind of hope.

Where are all the little tricks you recommend to others? Eh?

Paeonia martagen, lilies, oriental poppies. Can that crabapple support that vine? Can that cherry support that clematis and maybe a rampant and small white rose too? Dragged down. They might be. A burden eventually too weighty to struggle against.

Overbearing climber. Greedy, expedient clamberers. They never stop to doubt, self-doubt. At least it doesn't seem so.

Mozart, though, maybe has power over moods.

The mood-changing drugs? The chemicals that remember the momentary nature of so-called matter.

July 7, 1982

I seem to be getting garrulous like very young beginning poets drunk with the whole idea – so it all comes pouring out and you don't know which is useful, it all seems miraculous, marvellous, valuable.

But not real pearls. They are only produced by painful concentration, accumulation.

But still, don't scold. The Rose poem ran its full gestation period. Had a long painful parturition.

The exhilaration of the aftermath of its birth, encouraging me to keep my hand moving, pull out the matter lodged there in the mind and thought about, to which I've given a sneaky glance sometimes, or noticed a rumble deep down. And it's good exercise and it cleanses the contours of the imagination.

September 12, 1982 (In Edmonton)

The courage to be whoever you are. But *some* kind of connectedness is necessary – something to release things within. So isolated, how do they manage anything. I'm trapped in a limbo here, in a padded cell. A drink at the Faculty Club from 4:30–7 and then alone here – slightly drunk – nowhere to go, unsatisfied, the hum of alcoholic coitus interruptus. Fear and caution – the surface affability shatters away – doesn't come out to meet. I prowl around my thick carpeted rooms blank, caged. Turn on the radio, TV, get disgusted, O God O God. You're supposed to be getting on with your writing, they say. But I'm whirling around in sterile space. I'd do better in the vast formidable emptiness of Greenland's icy mountains that I saw from the aeroplane. Here, I was expecting people, planning how to keep them from eating up my life, was expecting to correct the excesses and temptations of an Ego Trip. Here I am about as far from an Ego Trip as it's possible to be. I miss the edgy desperation of other people with nervous systems like mine. I miss a neutral ground on which to communicate.

The sunsets, the sunrises, and one morning a gigantic rainbow without rain or sun. But the hideousness of the buildings, muddy parking lots, trim, unwitty parkland, and the University. One day I ventured a few yards down the ravine, looking for mushrooms – and found some – and felt happy to have things tearing my hair, and a whiff of the wilderness. Only two people have mentioned my work, but everybody refers to the *Books in Canada* piece, and the radio interview.

Time will unfold, no doubt.

But after expectation and excitement, to be suddenly alone, end-lessly, in this unreflecting apartment, or the wrong spurious office, hour after hour. And the kindness causes me only dismay – that one should *need* kindness seems wrong, a tinge of the insult, a feeling of being a chore. Pride is appalled.

Each person must find the necessary conditions for living, work-ing. So. Let me think. Such fundamentals were never missing before – even long ago in Ottawa, there were connections – with words, a few people. The problems were to remove alien pressures, intrusions, other people's takeovers.

This paralysis is different. A kind of love – with which I have been richly surrounded always, before. A support. How shall I remedy my lacks? How shall I make a working proposition for my work?

> Alone, alone, all, all alone
> Alone on a wide, wide sea!
> And never a saint took pity on
> My soul in agony![5]

I don't think I want to go into the past.
Pride is appalled.

The young girl patted the old woman's hand. There there, she said, be calm. We'll put a pretty ribbon in your hair and we'll sing a psalm.

To think! I was going to enrich their lives! And I find myself poverty-stricken. A desert within, a desert without. Needing *them* – if only they'd take pity on. Where can I find it, where is it hiding – the passion and the life?

Instead of the garden, what? (I'd hoped for the wilds.)

Instead of friends? (Kind acquaintances? – very different.)

Instead of big resolving tension drunks? (A civilized sip, stopped before one gets anywhere?)

Why this is Hell – and how shall I get out of it?

These terrible high-rises, a fearsome geometry – not the breathtaking arrogance of N.Y. skyscrapers – and the muddy (but dried out) parking lots – and the dominance of cars. And the endless flat pave-ments, wide uneventful roads.

It stands to reason, there must be a pulsing human life *somewhere*, here as elsewhere, there *must* be. Does it take place in their homes – visiting back and forth, tiny exchanges, boring each other for a purpose?

O where for me shall my salvation come, whence arrive? . . .

September 17, 1982

A few lightenings, liftings. But still mostly a whirl of nothingness.

Do I still *want* to write about mother? My children? Canada! Doubts.

The immediate is too important to leave for a moment.

September 20, 1982

Six months since Rose died.

An unattractive swagger that some old ladies have. They seem suffused with self-congratulations.

The little papery old men, not [illegible]. Aggression knocked out, they totter gratefully on.

'You've got to remember this is a Bible Belt,' said Olive (Dickenson).[6]

Corn belt. Celtic belt. Suspender belt.

They brought me, three of them, three used books: a local author, a child's history of north America, a history of the families (Ukrainian) who settled around Edmonton.

And muffins, rich nut and date bread, plums, tiny tomatoes, two large green tomatoes, two bottles of nice dry white wine.

The men grouped together and talked to each other. One, who came in alone, carrying his present in a brown paper bag, looked shy, alarmed, eyes scaredly avoiding mine, a faint goodwill trying to honour in place.

They had all, or mostly all, been to church before the strange 1:30 gathering.

September 26, 1982

I don't quite see how to use the Thirties Diaries. As they are, they're very raw. Rawness has some advantages, but . . .

Fifty years ago! The same me – but little Art. Maybe the emergence of? A bumpy history of growth?

True democracy here. And everybody seems so rich (well-off, I mean) – money no bother. Contented taxi-drivers and happy waitresses.

ND

A magpie flew through the blue and landed on the eccentrically shaped red brick and stayed still in profile, then walked along and dropped out of sight behind the brick, then reappeared, balanced on a pipe.

Red in front, to the left, tall geometric shapes in various shades of red. A painful nostalgic waiting brightness

March 15, 1983

Hanging by a thread.
Bleeding at both ends.
What's to be made of this long thin ship called Canada?
People still dreaming of the North.
Pushed toward Baffin Island. (Me too.)

All my vines, roses, creepers. All pulled down.
A naked edifice. I won't go back to that.
Exposed to the long brambly grass.

August 15, 1983 (Toronto)

It will come. Have faith. Amuse yourself. Think. Explore catharsis. Coddle and crack whip. Do not answer questions or think about them as asked. Take in only what's needed: a leaf, a continent, a blank hole.

October 28, 1983

The fragile vulnerability because of the Rose blow – welling up into any vacuum because of the piercing detail, and making so many words, sights, situations excruciating – and now it becomes more and more difficult to speak of this, while at first, and for a while, I could do naturally, sadly, but not so sadly it embarrassed the listeners. Pain crouches everywhere, in ambush, as I totter, unprotected, by.

Which makes any place to stand wobbly. Which makes lying down in sobriety dangerous. Which causes panic. So I stuff books in. Held together by safety-pins. (Visible in snaps – a face tortured but determined, held close, incommunicado – until? Some kind of deliverance. Juan says guilt is the slaying brute – but I'm not sure of that. That, or anything.[7])

Lately, tiny flashes of possibilities – that Baffin Island, a lost mother, the cruel Canadian, a dead child, death and decay within, far away and long ago, come together whirling with the luminous heart and lifting leaves in a strange new world.

Away. From where? Far. From what?

Long ago. When was that? And where will the jokes come from?

They chide me; which can only be out of a complete misunderstanding. (Yes, clever as they are.)

January 2, 1984 (The Dell)

Lonely and bored. Unstimulated. Blank. Reading, sleeping, eating, a brisk but desolate walk and becoming boring too.

Moaning, groaning, complaining, explaining, but not being able to explain. Getting fat, lethargic, hopeless, like an unloved child. Sorry for myself – for the *first* time ever.

I don't know *where* to go. I don't know *what* to do.

I feel trapped, caged.

Nobody's the least bit interested in me. (Me, as Me, me as other.) They're not even interested in my being interested in them.

Polite is all. If that. A tiresome kindness, for them, for me.

The telephone never rings.

November 1, 1984

It's getting desperate. Time gallops. Rivers run dry, etc., etc. Old Age and Death – Old Age and Death.

OK. That's OK. The fading away – not pretty, but natural.

Only I've left my duties so LATE. A thing not done . . .

ND

Sometimes I almost can explain why I do not want my writing to be like petit-point embroidery. Vehemently. But this does not mean that I do not enjoy or *appreciate* petit point, and the making of crafts.

It's the confusion of the two different things, one is an awesome entry into the meaning and seriousness of life – everybody lives. The other is a way of making time and surroundings pleasant.

There, idiot, that's clear enough for you, isn't it?

ROSE DIED

Unstoppable blossom
above my rotting daughter
Under the evil healing
bleeding, bleeding.

There was no way to explain
the Godly law: pain.
For your leaping greeting,
my failure, my betrayal,

shame for my cagey ways,
protective carapace;
blame for my greeting leaping
over your nowhere place.

Spring prods, I respond
to ancient notes that birds sing;
but the smug survivor says this is *after* the suffering,
a heavenly lift, an undeserving reward.

Your irreversible innocence
thought heaven now, and eternal,
was surprised, overwhelmed
by the painful roughly presented bill,

the hateful ways of the ungenerous.
But, loving the unsuspecting flower
could love urge bitchiness
as a safe protective covering?

O forgive, forgive, forgive,
as I know you would,
that my urgent live
message to you failed.

Two sins will jostle forever, and humble me
beneath my masked heart:
it was my job to explain the world;
it was my job to get the words right.

I tried, oh I tried, I did try,
I biked through gales,
brought hugs, kisses,
but no explanation for your despair, your desperate
                                    Why.

With its smile-protected face
my survival-bent person
is hurtled on by its nasty lucky genes,
its selfish reason,

and greets the unstoppable blossom
above my rotting daughter,
but forever and ever within
is bleeding, bleeding.

Elizabeth Smart

END NOTES

Chapter I: The Forties

1. Smart met Diana (Didy) Battye in the thirties in London when she had been a photographer's model. She was married to Michael Asquith, a serving naval officer, lived with her two children and was a neighbour of Smart.

2. Smart rented the bottom part of a house surrounded by an eight-foot wall, called College Farm, from the Fosters. Their daughter known as 'Big Girl' helped Smart with her children.

3. George Barker's *Eros in Dogma* published in 1943 is dedicated to his wife Jessica Barker.

4. Bobby McDougal was a friend from Ottawa.

5. Charles Ritchie was an Ottawa friend and one-time suitor who is now a Canadian diplomat. See *Necessary Secrets*, p. 94.

6. W S (Sydney) Graham, a Scottish poet who became a close friend of Smart's and had a wife called Nessie. He died shortly before Smart on January 9, 1986.

7. Frampton Meredith, a painter Smart had met in London in the thirties. See *Necessary Secrets*, p. 29.

8. George Barker's mother.

Chapter II: The Fifties

1. These entries were to be used in *The Assumption of the Rogues and Rascals*.

2. Paul Potts, a Canadian ex-patriate and writer living in London.

3. Artist Paddy Smith and his wife Oonagh were close friends of Smart's.

4. David Archer, a patron of poets, who ran the Parton Bookstore, a popular literary bookstore in London. Jean (Yanko) Varda, an artist now living in California. Smart had met Varda in Cassis, France and was living with him in California just before Barker arrived. Artist Julian Trevelyan and his wife Ursula, friends from London, with whom she went to Cassis. See *Necessary Secrets*, p. 87.

5. Graham Spry, founder of the Canadian Broadcasting Corporation and a close friend of Smart's. She had met him as a young girl, and he had encouraged her in her desire to write. See *Necessary Secrets*, p. 29.

6. Mike Pearson (Lester Bowles Pearson) and Charles Ritchie are friends from Ottawa. Pearson will become the Liberal Prime Minister of Canada from 1963 to 1968. Ritchie is a Canadian diplomat. See *Necessary Secrets*, p. 83.

7. The story of this fight between Smart and Barker on their return from a trip to Paris is well-known. He had hit her and she bit his lip.

8. Smart's eldest sister, Helen, died of cirrhosis of the liver.

9. Smart took amphetamines as a way of keeping herself going and to overcome bouts of what she called her lethargy, but which is probably the depressive phase of a manic-depressive syndrome.

Chapter III: The Sixties

1. Sholto, son of Mrs Watt, with whom Smart had sailed around the world as her companion. See *Necessary Secrets*, p. 27.

2. Experimental filmmaker William Mass, whom Smart had met with Barker in New York.

3. Jeffrey Bernard, friend and writer of the 'Low Life' column for the *Spectator*.

4. As Smart's garden grew, she gave names to its various areas.

The beargarden was so named because of a statue of a bear in it.

5. Clare and Julie became the respective wives of Christopher and Sebastian Barker. John is married to Georgina Barker.

6. Hetta Empson, wife of poet and critic William Empson, was a close friend of Smart's.

Chapter IV: The Seventies

1. Hubert Evans, a Canadian writer and friend.

2. Smart rented a cabin outside Kamloops, British Columbia, from Joan and Walter Winter. Little Sam is their son.

3. The metaphysical poets Henry Vaughan, George Herbert, and John Donne were among Smart's favourite poets.

4. Robert Burton's *Anatomy of Melancholy* (1621), an early study of melancholia, its causes, symptoms, and cures – or what we call depression.

5. The contents of this letter are not known, but Elizabeth and Jane, though close, were also always in competition with each other and intensely sensitive to each other.

6. A man from Porlock was said to have interrupted S T Coleridge after he had written the first eleven lines of 'Kubla Khan', thus destroying Coleridge's concentration, which explains the poem's deterioration after the first eleven lines.

7. Philoctetes, legendary Greek character, who on his way to the Trojan War was bitten by a snake and left by his companions to die on the island of Lemnos. He was brought back to Troy and healed after the oracle said the war could not be won without him.

8. Spark St., street in Ottawa where Smart grew up, synonymous with the capital city.

9. Claudia and Jane are Rose's daughters.

10. Smart's youngest and troubled daughter, Rose, had begun taking heroin, again.

11. Michael Asquith's second wife Hase.

12. Smart had worked a brief time writing for the women's page in the *Ottawa Journal* after she returned from France in the thirties. See *Necessary Secrets*, pp. 190–9.

13. *Let Us Dig a Grave and Bury Our Mothers*, published in *In the Meantime*, ed. Alice Van Wart (Toronto: Deneau, 1984). A novella based on the time she spent with the poet Alice Palaan and her husband, the surrealist Wolfgang Palaan, in New Mexico in the thirties. See *Necessary Secrets*, pp. 209–49.

14. Elizabeth Bowen, a well-known British writer of short stories.

15. She is working on completing *The Assumption of the Rogues and Rascals*, published later that year.

16. The title of her memoirs was to be 'Scenes One Never Forgets'.

17. Added by Elizabeth Smart at a later date.

18. She is referring to an incident that occurred on a boat trip she took with her father. She had become jealous of her father's attention to a woman he had met on the boat. See *Necessary Secrets*, pp. 71–81.

19. Erato, Polyphonia and Thalia are Greek mythological figures known as the muses. Erato is the goddess of lyric poetry or songs; Polyphonia is polyhymnia or goddess of mime; and Thalia is goddess of comedy.

20. British novelists Fay Weldon and Elaine Feinstein.

21. This 'motorway experience' was an incident in which Elizabeth almost died. A close male friend was driving her to the Dell after a party in Cambridge. They had a tiff and he forced her out of the car, leaving her in the snow with the temperature well below freezing. She may well have died had a Police car not rescued her. The man never apologized and their friendship ceased.

22. The writers are George Barker, Sydney Graham, David Gascoyne, Alan Simpson, Harold Pinter, John Barrington Wain and John Heath-Stubbs.

Chapter V: The Eighties

1. These works are now published in *In The Meantime* (Toronto: Deneau, 1984) as 'Dig a Grave and Let Us Bury Our Mothers', and 'Scenes One Never Forgets', along with selections from her final journals titled 'In the Meantime: Diary of a Blockage'. Smart's juvenile and garden journals are now also published in limited editions as *Smart's Juvenilia* (Toronto: Coachouse Press, 1987) and *Elizabeth's Garden Journals* (Toronto: Coachouse Press, 1988).

2. From Margaret Atwood's 'Soltise Poem' in *Two-Headed Poems* (1976).

3. Roly the dog was accidentally blinded.

4. Smart is using amphetamines for writing. Much of what she writes under their influence is incomprehensible.

5. Smart makes frequent allusions to Coleridge's 'Rime of the Ancient Mariner'.

6. Olive Dickenson, professor of history at the University of Alberta.

7. Juan Opez, Chilean musician and friend of Smart's in Toronto.

INDEX